THE
SUBMARINE BOOK

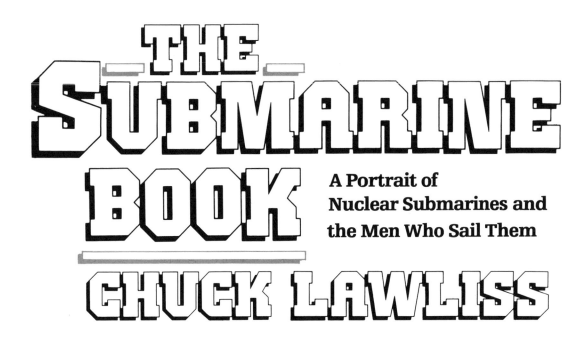

THE SUBMARINE BOOK

A Portrait of
Nuclear Submarines and
the Men Who Sail Them

CHUCK LAWLISS

THAMES AND HUDSON
New York and London

First published in the United States in 1991 by
Thames and Hudson Inc., 500 Fifth Avenue,
New York, New York 10110

First published in Great Britain in 1991 by
Thames and Hudson Ltd, London

Library of Congress Catalog Card Number
90-70393

Designed by Hugh O'Neill

Printed and bound in the United States of
America

CONTENTS

THE SUBMARINE BOOK

CHAPTER 1

"We know we're ready to attack"

At this moment, in secret places deep in the oceans of the world, down where the last traces of light vanish, huge U.S. Navy ballistic submarines are lying still in the water "on station," their nuclear missiles locked on key targets in the Soviet Union. Smaller, fast attack submarines, also nuclear-powered, are on constant patrol, often within a few miles of the coast of Russia, seeking Soviet submarines and monitoring their activities. Soviet submarines, ballistic and fast attack, are busy doing the same. Submarine fleets behave like rival street gangs, armed to the teeth, each protecting its turf while probing for a weakness in the enemy. Despite the changes sweeping the Soviet Union, perestroika and glasnost haven't eased the tension beneath the sea, nor do military experts feel that they will in the foreseeable future. The delicate balance of power beneath the sea still is an accepted fact of life in this, the fifth decade of the Atomic Age.

The mobility, secrecy, and sheer fire power of a ballistic submarine make it the most lethal weapon ever devised by man. The warheads on one ballistic missile submarine can destroy a dozen cities. If all the presently deployed American and Russian ballistic submarines fired their missiles on their predetermined targets, the world as we know it would end within the hour.

Little is known about nuclear submarines outside the military. A submarine is secretive by design. The submarine command of the U.S. Navy has been called the Silent Service, and the epithet is well deserved.

Little is known about the men who run the nuclear submarines, either. Much of what they do and what they experience at sea is secret, even from their families and friends. They are all males, all volunteers, above average in intelligence, better educated than most servicemen, and have a flair for mechanics or electronics. Many were computer freaks or Nintendo junkies before joining the Navy. They receive extra pay for serving aboard submarines, and they earn it.

A nuclear submarine can stay submerged for months, a long time to go without sunlight, fresh air, time off. It's a long time to go without family, girls, sports, sex, a cold beer. Life aboard a nuclear submarine is a continuous round of work, drills, sleep, and a minimum of quiet recreation in spaces that are claustrophobic at best. From the captain on down, everyone has enormous responsibilities, to one another, to the submarine and its nuclear power plant, to the missiles, to national defense. And danger lurks even in peacetime. Submarines, like airplanes, do not tolerate mistakes.

The nuclear submarine is a relatively new weapon, its resemblance to earlier submarines mostly superficial. Until years after World War II, the submarine wasn't even a true submarine, a vessel whose natural habitat is underwater. It was a diesel-powered vessel that could submerge and operate underwater for a limited time on battery power. When the batteries ran down, or the air gave out, it had to surface. Those are the characteristics of a submersible, not a submarine. The old submarines were armed with torpedoes, imperfect weapons at best. Despite these limitations, Hitler's submarines nearly drove Britain out of the war, and U.S. submarines were instrumental in the defeat of Japan.

In 1962 the first true submarine was launched, the nuclear-powered *Nautilus,* appropriately named after Jules Verne's fictional submarine. The *Nautilus* could do things that an earlier generation would have scorned as fantasy—travel underwater for months at a time, often at speeds in excess of thirty knots, sail around the world submerged, pass under the polar ice cap.

The next major development was inevitable: arm the nuclear-powered submarine with nuclear weapons. The first submarine missiles were crude, short-range, unguided, and inaccurate. But each generation of submarine-fired missiles was a giant step forward: Polaris, Poseidon, Tridents I and II progressively increased in range, explosive power, accuracy, and the ability to evade enemy detection while in flight.

These improvements brought about a change in the nuclear submarine's role in defense strategy. Conventional military wisdom once envisioned the following scenario for a nuclear war: the Soviet Union launches its missiles first; the United States discovers the launch before the Soviet missiles strike and launches a retaliatory attack;

both nations are nearly destroyed, neither is the winner. This bleak prospect was considered to be the ultimate deterrent to nuclear warfare.

At first, the U.S. retaliatory strike capacity consisted of ICBM (Intercontinental Ballistic Missile) silos and Strategic Air Command planes carrying nuclear bombs. Nuclear submarines were added to the mix when their missiles became capable of reaching Soviet targets with an adequate payload from an acceptable distance with reasonable accuracy.

The Strategic Balance in SSBNs

Country	Missile Type	Submarine Class	Number	Missiles per SSBN	Total Missiles
U.S.A.	Trident C-4	Ohio	8	24	192
		Lafayette / Franklin	12	16	192
	Poseidon C-3	Lafayette / Franklin	16	16	256
Total:			36		640
U.S.S.R.	SS-N-6	Yankee-I	18	16	288
	SS-N-8	Golf-III	1	6	
		Hotel-III	1	6	
		Delta-I	18	12	
		Delta-II	4	16	292
	SS-N-17	Yankee-II	1	12	12
	SS-N-18	Delta-III	14	16	224
	SS-N-20	Typhoon	4	20	80
	SS-N-23	Delta-IV	2	16	32
Total:			63		928

These figures, released by the Defense Department, represent the total number of ballistic missile submarines in the U.S. and U.S.S.R. fleets as of January 1, 1987. Despite a lower number of SSBNs, the United States has more of them at sea at any given time: 66 percent of its Ohio SSBNs and 55 percent of its Lafayette / Franklin SSBNs, a rough total of twenty. By comparison, the Soviet Union has averaged 13 percent of its ballistic missile submarines at sea.

Despite the disparity in the total number of missiles, the total effective yield in megatons is nearly the same: 1,484 megatons for U.S. missiles, 1,440 megatons for Soviet.

Ballistic submarines soon outgrew this supplementary role, when they achieved the ability to hit and destroy targets from nearly 2,000 miles away. Because ballistic submarines operate close to Russian shores, their missiles can reach Russian targets such as missile silos before missiles launched from SAC bombers or a silo. This is vital; seconds will be the margin of victory in a nuclear war. If nuclear war comes, the first shot probably will be fired by a ballistic missile submarine.

These huge SSBNs, "boomers" in Navy slang, are guarded by fast attack submarines while the SSBNs are on station. Fast attack submariners refer to the SSBNs as "hotels." A torpedoman explains, "They're big enough to be a hotel, and they just go out and park there for a couple of months."

Fast attack submarines are capable of diving to 1,475 feet and traveling submerged at speeds "in excess of thirty knots"; well in excess of thirty knots, according to military experts. They patrol right up to the Russian coast, and when Soviet submarines emerge stick with them wherever in the world they may go. If a warship or plane went as close to Soviet naval bases, it would create an international incident.

Killers as well as hunters, fast attack submarines are armed with strategic cruise missiles with ranges up to 1,500 miles. They also carry torpedoes, the traditional submarine weapon. Their Mark 48 torpedoes have a range of more than six miles and use on-board sonar to home in on a target. If the torpedoes miss, they attack again and again. Fast attack submarines can attack other submarines, surface ships, and land targets.

The crew of a fast attack submarine numbers 14 officers and 128 enlisted men, all superbly trained. It takes as long to earn the dolphins of a submariner as it does the wings of a pilot. After submarine school, an enlisted submariner spends up to a year in school learning to be a sonarman, torpedoman, electronics technician, or machinist's mate.

Getting aboard a fast attack submarine requires dexterity. Missiles, torpedoes, and supplies are lowered through hatches in the hull directly to their resting places, but humans climb down a narrow ladder on the side of the "sail," then down another ladder inside the submarine's pressure hull. The sail, called the conning tower on prenuclear submarines, is the equivalent of a ship's flying bridge, serving as the captain's command post while on the surface. Rising from the sail are a windshield, two periscopes, and a variety of antennas, all of which retract when the submarine submerges. Even cleats are turned upside down, their covers forming a smooth surface with the hull. An exposed cleat or an extended antenna creates noise. The biggest advantage of a submarine is not how fast or how deep it can go, but how silently.

On the surface, a submarine tosses and rolls; the hull is designed for running submerged, and no concessions are made for surface run-

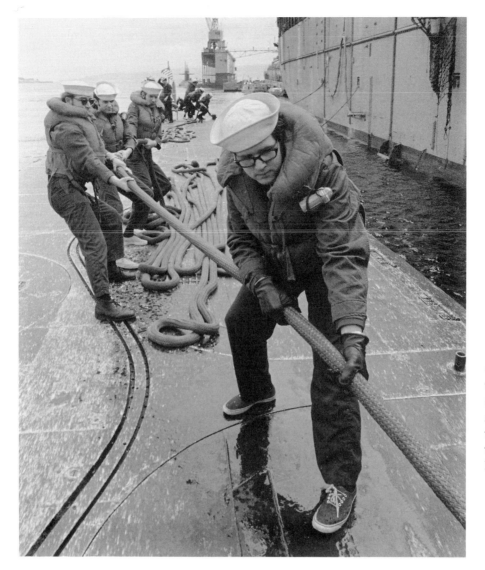

Crewmen shorten up lines on the deck of the ballistic missile submarine U.S.S. *John C. Calhoun* as she ties up alongside the tender U.S.S. *Canopus* at the big U.S. submarine base at Holy Loch, Scotland.

ning. There is little wake. Wake is turbulence, and turbulence is noise. Submarines leaving and entering their bases are monitored by Soviet spy satellites. A submarine's position is assumed to be known to the Soviets until after it crosses the edge of the continental shelf and dives deep.

A captain of a fast attack submarine says, "We pride ourselves on the ability to remain undetected, and the ability to inflict greater harm on someone than we would encounter. Actually, if we ever had to go to war, this is one of the safest platforms you could be on.

"I don't think I could operate in the private sector," he says. "When I assign somebody to do something, I expect it to be done to the standards we demand. There is no room for error. You can't come back and say, 'We installed the depth charges incorrectly,' or 'Sorry but we are going out on strike today.' Our safety, and the safety of our country, depend on us doing the job correctly.

"We know we are ready to attack. There is no doubt in my mind that if we had to go out and operate against an enemy, we'd fulfill our mission."

When it is time to dive, the men in the sail go below. A ladder leads down a narrow vertical pipe to the warm, well-lighted control room. On one side, two young sailors sit facing an array of digital readouts and electronic displays. They work steering wheels resembling those of light planes. One sailor, the helmsman, controls the horizontal course; the other, the planesman, controls the depth. Seated behind them quietly giving commands is the diving officer. Only the changing numbers on the depth gauge give evidence that the submarine is headed down under tons of cold seawater.

Every needed bit of information is on display somewhere in this thirty-by-thirty-foot room, and someone is monitoring each display. To the untrained eye, the scene is too complex to comprehend. To a submariner, it is simply an efficient way to check on the submarine's vital signs.

In the crowded control room of the nuclear-powered *Archerfish,* the two helmsmen keep a close eye on the ballast control panels as they maneuver the attack submarine in a dive to cruising depth.

One instrument seems out of place, so low-tech as to be an anachronism. It is the inclinometer, as uncomplicated as the glass part of a carpenter's level, which it resembles. The position of the bubble indicates the submarine's precise angle of incline or decline from horizontal. While diving or rising, the planesman must "keep the bubble" at exactly the degree called for. "I've lost the bubble" means "I'm confused and in trouble."

Sensors are needed because no visual information is available in a submerged submarine. The crew is sealed off from the sea. A surface ship heightens the senses; a submarine dulls them. A storm may be raging on the surface, but it doesn't intrude. The sense of movement and isolation is similar to being on a plane cruising at 35,000 feet. Indeed, a submarine behaves like a plane flying underwater.

Just aft of the control room is the sonar room. Bathed in a low green light, six operators sit in front of screens, watching sound as well as listening to it. What looks like luminous green sand drifts down their screens, each grain representing a blip of detected sound. Red and green lights glow on panels linking powerful computers with hydrophones outside the hull. Sonar enables the submarine to grope through the blackness of the depths, alert to anything nearby.

The ocean does strange things to sound waves. Sound travels more than four times as fast in water as it does in the air. Thermoclines, the boundaries between warm and cold layers of water, can reflect sound the way a mirror reflects light. Sometimes sound waves travel through water in straight lines, sometimes in arcs. Sound travels faster in warm water and in water under pressure. It will go down to the ocean floor, bounce up, then go back down again, in a manner similar to radio waves traveling in the air. Because of this property of sound waves, a ship may be detected at certain distances but not at others. Compared to sonar, radar is simple.

Computers are part of the equipment of a modern submarine. Among other functions, they process sonar data and translate it into fire control instructions. Despite the abundance of electronics aboard, U.S. naval policy discourages automation, believing that people make fewer mistakes than do machines, and can correct their mistakes faster. At a depth of 900 feet, a computer controlling the diving planes could malfunction and drive the submarine below crush depth in seconds, causing an implosion that would strew the wreckage for miles on the ocean floor. The Soviets, however, are automating many submarine functions, with the objective of smaller crews in smaller submarines.

All equipment is separated from the hull by thick rubber washers and rests on rubber cushions to reduce noise. The nuclear reactor produces steam to turn the turbines, and the turbines whine. The cooling pumps for the reactor, air conditioners, and compressors produce noise. To the degree the noise reaches the hull, it is transmitted into the ocean. Hydrophones on the exterior of the hull monitor the noise from inside the submarine. Accelerometers are used to detect any unnecessary vibration in rotating objects, and noisy parts are replaced immediately. A constant hum can be heard aboard, but careful design keeps it low.

The control room is the one place aboard where you can tell day from night. During daylight hours the overhead fluorescent lights are on. At sunset the room is "rigged for red," a number of tiny red lights come on, eerily illuminating the controls, accustoming the eye to the dark. Should the submarine surface quickly, the watch officer and others from the control room would go above the instant the sail broke the surface, and they can't spare precious moments adjusting to the dark. Leaving the control room at night, watch personnel wear red goggles to retain night vision.

A third of the crew is nearly always asleep. Berthing areas are lit by dim red lights. The other working areas are lit all the time. Day and night lose their meaning. The passage of time is measured by work, sleep, and meals.

As there is no sense of night and day, there is no sense of the sea-

A headset brings music to a crewman relaxing in his bunk aboard the U.S.S. *Francis Scott Key*. Living quarters are cramped aboard a submarine. Only the captain has a room of his own.

son. The temperature and humidity aboard are kept at a uniform, comfortable level. And no sense of weekends or holidays, since the routine never varies.

Space is at a premium. The aft half of the submarine is engineering space, housing the reactor and the turbines. In the bow: missiles, torpedoes, and sonar equipment. Every nook and cranny has something in it. The cream-colored bulkheads and passageways are lined with cables and pipes, and sprinkled with valves and gauges. Sailors must turn sideways to pass one another. Taller sailors constantly duck to avoid banging their heads.

Only the captain has his own cabin, as small as a single compartment on a train. The bunk folds up to provide him with a small desk. The other officers live three to an equally small cabin, their bunks stacked three-up, the lowest at floor level.

An enlisted man sleeps on a bunk, or "rack," three feet by six feet with a twenty-six-inch clearance, and it is difficult for a big man to roll over. On the bunks are camouflage blankets of a synthetic material. "They don't make lint," an officer explains. "We used to have wool blankets, but the lint clogged the air filters." Beneath the bedding under a plywood cover is a four-inch-deep locker where the sailor keeps his worldly goods. In each bunk space are earphone jacks to plug into an entertainment system offering several types of music. A religious channel is popular, perhaps because no services are held aboard.

"A sailor's bunk is really his kingdom," an officer explains. "It's the only spot that's really his, his little niche. When he gets upset and has to get away from it all, he can't go topside and take a walk on deck."

There are ninety-six bunks for enlisted men, and often there are more sailors aboard than that. Some bed down in the torpedo room, some use air mattresses anywhere there's sufficient floor space. For others it means hot-racking: three men for every two racks, sleeping in shifts.

Submarine duty is tough, and captains try to make things easier for the crew. Uniform regulations are more relaxed than in any other branch of the service. The crew wears blue or black coveralls, called "poopie suits," and running shoes, or "topsiders."

The crew receives no mail while on patrol, but familygrams are relayed by radio. A sailor gives a pad of familygrams to his parents, wife, or girl friend, and he may receive a total of eight forty-word messages while at sea. There are no outgoing personal messages of any kind; radio transmissions are too easily detected.

Submarines occasionally will pull into a foreign port and the crew will be given liberty. If that's not on the schedule, the captain may bring the submarine up to periscope depth and let a few sailors look through it briefly, a treat called "periscope liberty."

The nuclear age brought many improvements to the life of a submariner, but none so welcome as plentiful fresh water. A World War

II submariner on patrol might be allowed one or two showers a week; today showers are a daily affair. The shower routine, however, remains the same: get in, turn on the water, get wet, turn off the water, soap up, turn on the water, rinse, turn off the water.

Submariners still grow beards at sea, but they must be shaved off at the end of the patrol. A beard contest usually is held aboard toward the end of the patrol. And some submariners still have the dolphins and conning tower symbol tattooed on their arms.

At the start of a patrol, the crew seems easygoing and congenial, but about two weeks out, edginess begins. Some sailors become irritable and snappish; they calm down and others start in—all as predictable as the tide. Another predictable phenomenon: the crew will get silly the final days at sea. The Navy calls this "channel fever."

No psychiatrist is aboard, not even a doctor. The physical well-being of the captain and crew is the responsibility of a senior pharmacist mate, trained to operate independently. Medical equipment and supplies are stowed in a space the size of a hall closet. Should someone be critically sick or severely injured, the pharmacist mate may recommend to the captain that the submarine be brought to the surface so that he can consult with a Navy doctor by radio, or that the man be evacuated by helicopter. The final decision rests with the captain.

Like nuclear-powered surface ships, submarines generate power and produce fresh water. But submarines also make their own air. Special generators produce oxygen by electrically hydrolyzing water. The air aboard is monitored constantly for contaminants and the proper mix of gases, oxygen, carbon dioxide, and nitrogen. A complex mechanism continuously "scrubs" the air of carbon dioxide. A by-product of this process is gaseous hydrogen, which is expelled into the ocean through a diffuser, since big bubbles might be visible on the surface.

No aerosol sprays are allowed on board—no cans of deodorants, shaving cream, lighter fluid, shoe polish, or paint that can adversely affect the ozone level. Yet sailors may smoke aboard, in places and at times designated by the captain. The Navy is committed to being smoke-free within the next five years but still has a way to go.

A fast attack submarine puts to sea with sufficient food for sixty days. Each day the crew consumes twenty-five loaves of bread, twenty-eight gallons of milk, and ten pounds of coffee. The bread is baked aboard; dough takes less room to store than packaged loaves. Foodstuff is stored in sequence so that the ingredients for each day's menu are always close at hand. At the beginning of a patrol, the freezer and dry-goods storage areas are full, and the overflow of canned goods spills into the crew's mess. Submariners have to walk over their food until they eat their way through it.

The fresh food—fruits, vegetables, milk—are gone before the patrol is half over, and the cook switches to food that has been frozen, dehydrated, or canned. If a nuclear submarine didn't run out of food, it could stay submerged indefinitely. Garbage on a submerged subma-

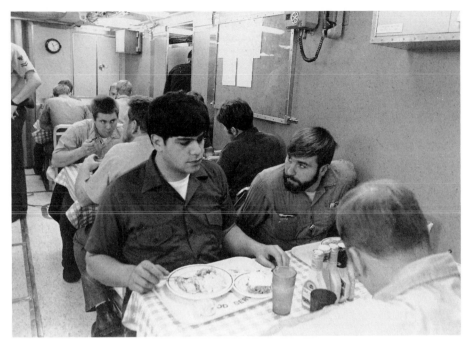

Some of the crew of the U.S.S. *Ohio* chow down in the mess hall of the submarine during precommissioning trials. To compensate for other hardships, food aboard submarines is the best in the Navy.

rine goes out the TDU (Trash Disposal Unit), a vertical tube that ejects packaged garbage, weighted to sink to the bottom.

Submarine food is considered the best in the Navy. Meals are served from the stove, not a steam table, and there is table service, not a chow line. There isn't room to do it any other way. "Our cooks are vital to morale," the captain says. "If a sailor has a crummy meal, he's going to be grouchy all day."

Or all night. A meal is served every six hours; the midnight meal is called "midrats." In addition, a sailor can go in the galley and make a sandwich any time he wants and help himself to coffee, milk, sodas, a fruit punch called "bug juice," and soft ice cream. Between meals the mess, the only open area on the submarine, serves as a lecture and training area, a study and reading room, an entertainment center, and a place to shoot the breeze. No alcoholic beverages are allowed aboard U.S. submarines.

Officers eat the same food as the enlisted men, but in the tiny officers' mess and with a touch of class. Stewards wear short red jackets and behave as formally as waiters in a fine restaurant. The officers' wardroom also leads a double life as meeting room and recreation area. And should the pharmacist mate have need of an operating table, the wardroom table is at his disposal.

Among the busiest sailors aboard are those fresh from submarine school, still earning their silver dolphins. These "non-quals" are taught firsthand how a submarine operates, a learning process that may take a year. The training is intense. Submariners must know every major system aboard, be able to describe how it works, draw it, and recite its parameters: what alarms are associated with what systems, and where the overrides are for all the hydraulic valves.

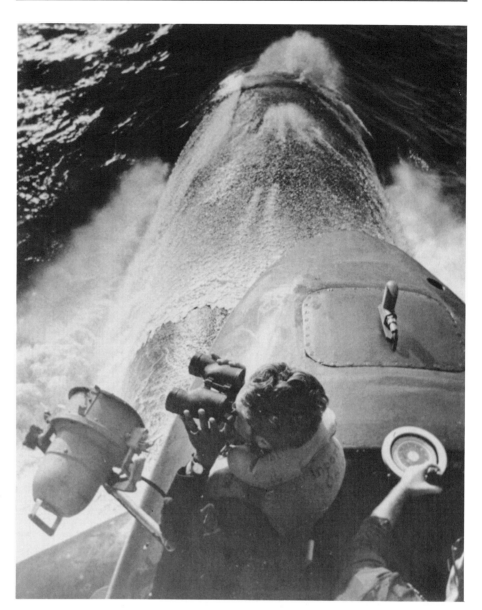

A crewman scans the horizon from the sail of the U.S.S. *Daniel Boone.* Nuclear-powered submarines have no need to surface except when entering or leaving port or when visual checks are needed.

It isn't unusual, according to a chief petty officer, for some men to work almost nonstop for twenty-four or thirty hours while under way. "The sacrifices that men make on fast attack submarines are unbelievable," he says. "They get damn little time off. They average, I would say, sixty to eighty hours a week when we're in port. Last year we were away from our home port seventy per cent of the time. We have a schedule, but on a fast attack it's set in quicksand. We've got more things to cover than we've got submarines. We got an emergency call in one day that said we were going out the next morning. We didn't know how long. It was forty-odd days later when we finally pulled in."

Besides the work, the training, and the watches, there are daily drills. The claxon blares. The nature of the "emergency" is announced on the intercom: fire in the reactor room, flooding in the torpedo room,

The array of instruments in the control room of the attack submarine *Whale* controls her ballast tanks. Every function of a submarine is constantly monitored under the watchful eyes of the crew.

The U.S.S. *Woodrow Wilson* blows her ballast tanks in a shipyard test. Like their early predecessors, modern submarines dive and rise to the surface by filling and blowing their ballast tanks.

a crash dive. Sleepers roll out of bed and join the men racing to their stations. Submariners learn to go to sleep fast and wake up fast. Every drill is timed. In a real emergency, a few seconds can mean the difference between life and death.

There is little time for recreation and it is mostly electronic. There are movie cassettes, one for each day of the patrol, a personal computer with a selection of video games, a small library. Some sailors bring their hobbies aboard. A torpedoman sketches his shipmates. A machinist's mate builds a sailing ship in a bottle. Traditionalists play cards.

Exercise equipment is tucked into nooks and crannies. A rowing machine. Barbells. A stationary bicycle. A workout is an antidote to the enforced immobility of submarine life. There are no sun lamps, however. Submariners are always pale.

Submariners, like all armed services members, must stay in shape and pass semiannual tests comprised of sit-ups, pull-ups, and a timed distance run. They also must keep their weight below proscribed levels. Those failing to meet the minimum standard are put on a training regimen; to fail twice usually means returning to civilian life.

No other part of the armed forces has more top secret equipment or performs more top secret missions. Exciting things happen on patrol that submariners can't talk about. The submarine command discourages publicity, but submariners do speak candidly about some aspects of their lives.

Submariners are elitists. They see themselves as a cut above the rest of the Navy. An electronics technician says, "I never want to go to sea on a skimmer [a submariner's term for a surface ship]. Hey, there are only two kinds of ships—submarines and targets."

But even elitists have problems. One married submariner relates, "My daughter, she's three, says, 'Daddy, don't go to work. Please don't.' And when I come back, for the first week she won't come to me. It's nerve-racking." Another says, "It's like getting a divorce twice a year." His friend chimes in, "Hey, I think it's like going on a honeymoon twice a year." Everyone laughs.

A young radioman complains, "My wife said to me, 'Look, sweetheart, either you're married to me or you're married to that goddamn sub. Which is it?' "

A major strain on a marriage is that while the man is at sea his wife becomes accustomed to making all the decisions. When he comes home, he takes charge, or attempts to. By the time things have settled down, he's off again.

The divorce rate in the Navy is the highest of all the services, still higher among submariners. Some 20 percent of enlisted submariners leave the service every year. The Navy does what it can to promote domestic tranquillity. When family problems arise, there are places to turn to. An ombudsman is available at every naval station to interface between the Navy and families. The wives of submariners are a close-knit, mutually supportive group.

Despite the problems, despite the hardships, these men genuinely like being submariners. They like feeling they are personally important to the ship's mission. Many seem to imply, "See how tough this duty is, and I *volunteered*. I'm tough, too. I can take it, and I keep coming back for more."

They also like being part of a team. To operate a submarine demands teamwork of the highest order. But it goes beyond that. The crew of a submarine is an archetypal example of male bonding, and male bonding eases the hardship, soothes the loneliness, and makes the unthinkable bearable. The dangers seem less threatening because they are shared. The moral burden imposed by the lethal missiles aboard is diluted by sharing, and by fixing the responsibility elsewhere. A fire controlman, questioned about the ultimate consequences of his job, spoke in platitudes until his patience was exhausted, then snapped, "*We* don't fire the missiles. The *President of the United States* fires the damn missiles!"

Navy Terms

anchor watch	seamen available for night work
binnacle	stand or enclosure for a compass
burdened vessel	vessel required to take action to avoid collision
cat's paw	puff of wind
comber	deep-water wave
confused sea	rough sea without pattern
conshelf	continental shelf
dead reckoning	method of navigation using direction and amount of progress from the last well-determined position to a new position
dead water	thin layer of fresher water over a deeper layer of more saline water
deep scattering layer	ocean layer that scatters sound or echoes sound vertically
degaussing	reduction of magnetic field of a ship to protect against magnetic mines
density layer	layer of water in which density changes sufficiently to increase buoyancy
dodger	canvas windshield on exposed bridge
dog	metal fitting used to close ports and hatches
following sea	waves moving in the same general direction as the ship
fracture zone	an area of breaks in underwater rocks, such as sea mounts, ridges, troughs
freshet	an area of fresh water at mouth of a stream flowing into the sea
frogmen	underwater demolition personnel
gig	ship's boat for use of the commanding officer
hangfire	delayed detonation of an explosive charge
hull down	said of a ship slightly visible on horizon
internal wave	wave that occurs within a fluid whose density changes with depth

kedge	to move a ship by means of a line attached to a small anchor (also called a kedge) dropped at the desired position
lighter	bargelike vessel used to load or unload a ship
officer of the deck	officer in charge who represents the captain
order of battle	disposition of ships as they ready for combat
phantom bottom	false sea bottom registered by electronic depth finders
Q-ship	disguised man-of-war used to decoy enemy submarines
rips	turbulent agitation of water, generally caused by interaction of currents and wind
rough log	original, pencil-written version of the ship's log
salinity	quantity of dissolved salts in seawater
scupper	fittings on weather decks that lead water to drain overboard
strakes	continuous lines of fore and aft planking
target bearing	compass direction of a target from a firing ship
tender	logistic support and repair ship
trick	helmsman's watch at the wheel
yaw	of a ship, to rotate about her vertical axis

Submarine Acronyms

ARD	U.S. Navy designation for a floating dry dock
ARS	submarine salvage vessel
ASDIC	British equivalent of sonar
ASW	antisubmarine warfare
BIBS	Built-In Breathing System; emergency breathing equipment in sea-floor habitat
DDC	Deck Decompression Chamber
DDS	Deep Diving System; surface-ship system providing all necessary equipment for a diver to descend, perform a mission, and return to the surface
DSSP	Deep Submergence Systems Project
IX	designation for an unclassified miscellaneous vessel
LORAN	LOng-RANge electronic navigation
SLBM	submarine-launched ballistic missile
SS	designation for U.S. Navy submarine
SSB	fleet ballistic missile submarine
SSBN	fleet ballistic missile submarine—nuclear-powered
SSG	guided missile submarine
SSGN	guided missile submarine—nuclear-powered
SSK	antisubmarine submarine
SSN	fast attack submarine
SST	target submarine
TDC	torpedo data computer

CHAPTER 2

"The destruction of her country's enemies"

Submarines and submariners are both made in the New London, Connecticut area and have been since 1900 when the Navy reluctantly decided to buy its first submarine. Nuclear submarines are built along the Thames River in Groton, Connecticut at the Electric Boat Division of General Dynamics. Submariners are trained on the river nearby at the Naval Submarine Base. Submarines operate out of here, and the base provides a variety of special services to the submarine fleet. Some 15,000 sailors are stationed here, all either submariners or involved with submarines in some way. Submarines are what New London is all about. The launching of a new submarine is a joyous civic event.

Electric Boat built the Navy's first submarine in 1900 and has the design contract for the propulsion system of the Seawolf class, the next generation of attack submarines, which will be operable around the turn of the century. This is big business. The annual payroll at Electric Boat is more than 624 million dollars.

Electric Boat built seventy-four submarines during World War II and supervised the building of twenty-eight others. It built the *Nautilus,* the first nuclear submarine, in the early 1950s. Since then, the company has designed fifteen of the eighteen classes of the Navy's submarines. It has built twenty-four of the thirty-eight Los Angeles-class attack submarines, and all of the Tridents.

Currently two classes of submarines are being built at Electric Boat, fast attack submarines (SSNs) and ballistic missile submarines (SSBNs). A fast attack submarine is a tube of two-inch-thick steel weighing 6,135 tons, 360 feet long with a 33-foot beam. It displaces 6,900 tons submerged and carries a crew of 142.

Ballistic missile submarines, the Ohio-class Tridents, are 560 feet long (15 feet longer than the Washington Monument is high), measure 42 feet at the beam, displace 18,700 tons submerged, and carry a crew of 165.

Tridents, called boomers by submariners, are fitted with twenty-four ballistic missiles (SLBMs), which can be launched while submerged. Each missile is fitted with eight, and potentially twelve, nuclear warheads. A Trident can deliver a total payload of 19.2 megatons, 1,280 times the power of the atomic bomb that fell on Hiroshima. There were eight Tridents in the mid-1980s, carrying a total of 192 SLBMs with 1,536 warheads.

There are another twenty-eight ballistic missile submarines in the older Lafayette, James Madison, and Benjamin Franklin classes, most of them built by Electric Boat. Collectively they have 5,472 nuclear warheads, a total deliverable explosive force of 403.2 megatons.

Beginning with the ninth Trident, the U.S.S *Tennessee* (SSBN-734), launched in December 1986, new SSBNs carry the D-5 weapon system, an array of 6,000-mile SLBMs with the accuracy and explosive power to hit and destroy the hardest missile enforcements.

A ballistic submarine is a mobile missile silo. After leaving port, she proceeds to a secret point in the ocean where she is on station, staying submerged there for sixty or seventy days. Each SSBN has two crews, a blue and a gold, complete from captain on down, which alternate tours at sea. This arrangement gives the Navy full utilization of its SSBNs. To meet demanding deployment schedules, crews fly to and from SSBN bases. There is a short period when the crews overlap, allowing the fresh crew to be briefed firsthand on the status of all the equipment and systems aboard.

The Naval Submarine Base was founded in 1916, and every submariner, officer or enlisted man, who ever served aboard a Navy submarine learned his trade at the submarine school here. Other related commands share the 1,325-acre base: Submarine Group Two, comprising three squadrons of fast attack submarines; the submarine tender *Fulton;* the submarine rescue ship *Sunbird;* a number of schools offering training in specialized submarine skills; a hospital; the Submarine Medical Research Laboratory; the Naval Medical Underseas Institute; and a submarine museum.

Submarine officers come from three sources: the naval academy at Annapolis, the Naval Reserve Officer Candidate program (NROTC), and the Nuclear Propulsion Officer Candidate program (NUPOC), open to college juniors and seniors. Before being accepted, every candidate is interviewed three times: a personal screening by a vice admiral and two technical interviews with senior engineering officers.

Submarines tied up at the naval
base in New London, Connecticut, the unofficial U.S. submarine capital. Submarines are
built here and operate out of
here, and submariners are
trained here.

The attack submarine U.S.S.
Key West slides down the ways
after being christened at the
Electric Boat Company yard in
New London, Connecticut. The
launching ceremony is a festive
occasion.

The NUPOC men go to Newport, Rhode Island, for Officer Candidate School, a four-month indoctrination into naval command. Upon graduation they are commissioned and join the Annapolis and NROTC officers for a year of advanced nuclear power training. It starts with twenty-six weeks of classroom training at the Nuclear Power School (NPS) at Orlando, Florida, and includes courses in advanced mathematics, physics, chemistry, electrical engineering, reactor theory, and thermodynamics, a total of 687 classroom hours. About one thousand officers go through this program each year.

Then comes twenty-four weeks of hands-on training at one of the Navy's three reactor training facilities in Idaho Falls, Idaho; Windsor Locks, Connecticut; or Ballston Spa, New York. After learning the systems and components of a nuclear plant, the officers train on a full-scale operating replica of a nuclear propulsion plant, and related systems.

Future submarine officers go to New London to attend the Naval Submarine School, where in thirteen weeks they will acquire the basic knowledge and skills needed by a submarine officer. Those who will serve on nuclear-propelled aircraft carriers and cruisers go to the surface warfare officer school.

All officers aboard a submarine except the supply officer are specialists in nuclear propulsion. Some authorities believe this concentration on engineering does not produce effective submarine captains. Tom Clancy, the author of the submarine thriller *The Hunt for Red October,* says:

> Agreement in the submarine community—in private—is almost universal, the Royal Navy produces better commanding officers. Those aspiring to command are trained to one thing: operate the submarine and hit targets. The Royal Navy's engineers are not allowed to command. The American system requires that a submarine officer spend too much time in the engine room. A submarine is not an excuse to build a nuclear reactor. A submarine is a weapon of war whose only purpose is the destruction of her country's enemies.

Upon graduation from submarine school, an officer begins his apprenticeship aboard a submarine in one of several billets: damage control assistant, main propulsion assistant, electrical officer, or reactor controls assistant.

When the captain decides that the officer has completed his apprenticeship satisfactorily, usually after six to eight months, he invites the commodore of the sub group and two other officers aboard. They question the officer to make sure he is proficient in his duties. The commodore interviews him to make sure he has the proper mental attitude and motivation to be a career submarine officer. If he passes muster, the dolphin insignia is pinned on his uniform. All qualified submariners, officers and enlisted men, wear the dolphin insignia.

The officer now is a full lieutenant and ready for more responsibility. Possible assignments include: communicator, the officer responsible for the conduct and supervision of radio communications; first

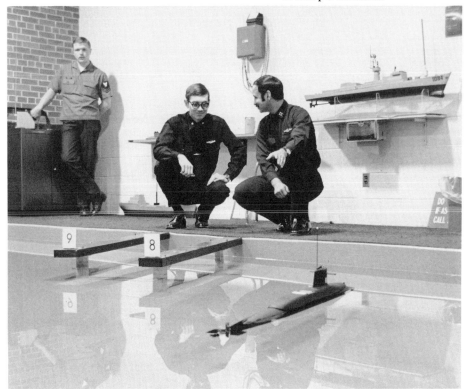

Two submarine officers use a radio-controlled model to refresh their skills at bringing a submarine to a pier. Periodic refresher training is part of being a submariner, whether officer or enlisted man.

An instructor at the submarine school in New London, Connecticut demonstrates submarine trimming techniques. Graduates must serve an apprenticeship aboard a submarine before being awarded the dolphin insignia.

MAX LOAD LIMIT 7

In a New London, Connecticut drydock the *Ohio* SSBN-726 is readied for her first patrol. The efficiency of the submarine fleet depends on keeping to a bare minimum the amount of time a submarine is in port.

At its launching at the Electric Boat yard in New London, Connecticut, the sleek U.S.S. *Phoenix,* a fast attack submarine, slides past three ballistic missile submarines in various stages of construction.

lieutenant, responsible for the operation and maintenance of the ship's deck and the maintenance of the external hull; sonar officer, responsible for the conduct and supervision of underwater search; missile and missile fire control officer, responsible for operating, maintaining, and targeting missiles; torpedo and torpedo fire control officer, with similar responsibilities for torpedoes; and launching officer, responsible on SSBNs for the missile launcher subsystem. A knowledge of all these assignments is a prelude to command.

As an officer progresses, the Navy moves him around to broaden his background. After a tour of sea duty, he may be an instructor in one of the specialized schools or on the staff of a submarine group, then go to sea on a different class of submarine. If he earned his dolphins on a fast attack submarine, he'll be assigned to a boomer.

All dream of commanding their own submarine. Those who make it are commanders in their middle or late thirties who have served as executive officers. A prerequisite to command is graduation from Prospective Commanding Officer (PCO) school.

A submarine captain serves one or, in exceptional instances, two three-year tours, then moves on to other command duties. It's not that captains burn out; their command time is limited by the number of qualified officers waiting to take their place.

Like submarine officers, enlisted submariners are an elite group. To qualify for enlisted nuclear training a young man must be between seventeen and twenty-five, a high school graduate, and score high on Navy aptitude tests. Beyond the normal medical standards, he must have normal color vision and be free of any congenital ailment, even acute acne. Submarine duty no longer has a special height limitation; submariners may be as tall as six feet six, the limit for all Navy personnel.

Every nuclear field recruit spends eight weeks of basic training at Orlando learning what the Navy is all about. Then he goes to one of the three specialty schools—mechanical, electrical, or reactor operator—for thirteen to thirty weeks.

For those who will become qualified nuclear operators, the next step is the Nuclear Power School for twenty-four weeks learning the theory and operation of a nuclear propulsion plant. The subjects, most taught at college level, include mathematics, physics, chemistry, heat transfer and fluid flow, reactor principles, reactor plant technology, and radiological fundamentals.

This is a demanding course, comparable to the one given to officers at their nuclear power school, and enlisted men of exceptional promise are encouraged to apply for either Annapolis or the NROTC program. Graduates of the enlisted men's Nuclear Power School go next to a nuclear power training unit (NPTU) to spend twenty-six weeks qualifying as a propulsion plant operator on a land-based prototype reactor plant.

Most NPTU graduates then go to submarine school, the others to nuclear-powered surface ships. However, not all enlisted submariners are graduates of NPTU. Sonarmen, radiomen, torpedomen, and cooks, for example, are trained in specialized schools and learn the

The largest U.S. submarine ever built, 560 feet long and 36 feet 6 inches at the beam, the *Ohio*, SSBN-726, is rolled out of the assembly building and onto a pier at Electric Boat's Groton, Connecticut yard.

basics of nuclear propulsion while aboard submarines.

A psychological screening test is given to determine a candidate's ability to cope with the stresses of life aboard a nuclear submarine. The test is designed to detect potential problems: suicidal tendencies, persecution complexes, latent paranoia, claustrophobia. If any abnormality is indicated, a Navy psychiatrist will evaluate the candidate to determine if he should be allowed to continue submarine training.

The test was developed and refined over the years by the Submarine Medical Research Laboratory. It has a staff of eighty, a quarter of whom are Ph.D.s. The commander, Captain Claude A. Harvey, is a Navy doctor who has spent time on seventeen different submarines in the course of his research.

"Very few are rejected from submarine school for psychological problems," Captain Harvey explains. "The reason is that a lot of self-screening has taken place before the man gets here. Someone who is terrified of being shut up in a small space doesn't volunteer for submarine duty. And rarely does someone with a psychiatric disorder

The crew of a submarine takes part in an emergency breathing apparatus drill. Constant drills are a necessary part of submarine life to ensure instant and correct reaction in case of an emergency.

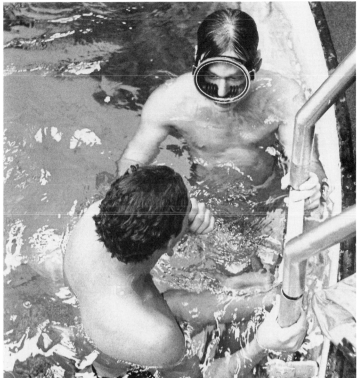

A Navy diver instructs a submarine school student in the
"blow/go" method of escaping
from a stricken submarine. Submariners must be strong swim-
mers and feel at home in and
under the water.

The air pressure is increased to
a painful level in tests in the
tank at the submarine school.
To escape from a stricken submarine, a crewman must be
able to withstand the pressure
of the deep.

An instructor watches a young
sailor scramble from the pressure chamber at the submarine
school. To qualify, a candidate
must stand up to mental and
psychological as well as physical pressure.

have the motivation to get through the intensive training that precedes submarine school. Submarine volunteers almost invariably want to prove something to themselves, and they possess a high degree of self-discipline.

"It's hard to be on a submerged submarine for a long time," he says, "but not that much harder than being at sea for a comparable time on a surface ship. Go below decks on a cruiser or a carrier, the space is almost as confining as on a submarine. The only difference is that the man can't go up on deck to get away from it all and feel the sun on his face."

A submariner, he explains, is kept busy, usually with intellectually demanding tasks. "When he has finished his watch, he's tired, and because he's tired he's less apt to react negatively to his environment. We're herd animals. If we see others adapting, we're more apt to adapt ourselves. The senior petty officers, the old hands, if you will, have a calming effect on those who are making their first patrol.

"As to the length of time they are submerged, surprisingly, it doesn't make a difference," he says. "If a man is going to be disturbed by being on a submarine, he'll be disturbed quite early on. In other words, tension doesn't seem to build; any pressures in that direction are mitigated by the adaptive process he is undergoing. A man suffering a breakdown aboard a submarine is as rare as, say, a man with a ruptured appendix."

When nuclear submarines were first built, the Submarine Medical Research Laboratory ran an experiment, Project Hideout, to determine how long a crew could stay submerged. A crew, accompanied by laboratory observers, went aboard a docked submarine and performed their duties without coming out, just as if they were at sea. The experiment was called off after sixty days because all the food had been eaten. The crew was tired, but no psychological problems had surfaced.

What is the ideal personality for a submariner? The answer, apparently, is that there is none. Captain Harvey explains: "One would think that Type A personalities would make the best submariners. Full of energy, outgoing, take-charge guys. But in World War II, when a submarine would be taking a terrific pounding from depth charges, the lights out, filled with diesel fumes, the Type A's didn't fare too well. They burned out, became phlegmatic. It was the Type B's, the quiet, introspective men, who took charge and did the things that had to be done.

"It doesn't sound very scientific to say that we need all types of personalities—normal personalities—aboard a submarine, but it's true. Scientifically proven, at least to the Navy's satisfaction."

The crew of a ballistic missile submarine has a particular psychological burden, the knowledge that they may someday have to rain destruction on helpless cities. This is an awesome responsibility for young men to live with.

"The men talk among themselves about this," Captain Harvey says.

"Certainly it is on their minds. But they sincerely believe that they represent a deterrent to nuclear warfare, not a provocation. The psychological protection they employ is to believe they never will have to do it—and they are almost certainly correct. If an SSBN ever fires, she will have failed in her job. The Navy will have failed in its job.

"There's something else that should be understood about SSBNs. Any command to fire must come encoded by radio. Several officers would be involved in decoding the message. All must agree that an order to fire has been given, and all must agree to fire. The ship must be brought to the proper depth for firing. All this involves so many officers and men that there is no way a missile can be launched by a crazed captain, or by a few crazed crewmen, for that matter."

The laboratory is currently working on several projects. One is developing programs to assist submarine pharmacist mates in making diagnoses. Another explores ways to help sonarmen and radarmen read the displays on their machines more accurately. This is a subject close to Captain Harvey's heart.

"After the *Vincennes* [a U.S. cruiser] shot down the [Iranian] airliner in the Persian Gulf, much criticism centered around radar operators not being able to properly read what is on their screen, no way to tell the good guys from the bad guys. Let me assure you that considerable time and money goes into making operators more proficient, and making the displays easier to read. The funding for our project, for example, is in excess of a million a year."

The nearby Naval Underseas Medical Institute has an enviable reputation for applied research. Among its accomplishments: international use of the color orange for life jackets and buoys; the Falant Test, the definitive process for determining normal color vision; and the red lighting aboard submarines used to enhance night vision. The institute now is experimenting with very low intensity white light to facilitate chart reading without impairing night vision.

Near the institute on the bank of the river is the New London area's major tourist attraction, the Nautilus Memorial/Submarine Force Library & Museum, attracting more than a quarter of a million visitors a year. They approach the museum through a bronze arch, a replica of a hull ring of an Ohio-class submarine, a 43-foot reminder of just how big ballistic submarines are. On the grounds are some vintage submarines, including Simon Lake's *Explorer* and a Japanese midget submarine.

In the entrance hangs an eleven-foot model of Jules Verne's fanciful *Nautilus*. Inside are working periscopes, a World War II control room, and a wall of models depicting the development of the submarine. Two minitheaters show short movies depicting the history of the submarine and the career of the real *Nautilus,* decommissioned in 1980 and moved here in 1985. Visitors may go below on the *Nautilus* and tour the control room and crew's quarters. The first of the nuclear submarines looks surprisingly dated, resembling the submarines of World War II as much as it does the submarines of today.

Commissioning Pennant

Naval lore has it that when the Dutch were at war with England in the seventeenth century, a Dutch admiral hoisted a broom at his masthead to symbolize his intention to sweep the English from the sea. This gesture was answered by Admiral William Blake, who hoisted a horsewhip to indicate his intention to chastise the Dutch. The victorious English thus set the precedent for a long, narrow commissioning pennant symbolizing the original horsewhip as the distinctive emblem of a ship of war.

Submarines in the Movies

Around the World Under the Sea. Frogman Lloyd Bridges plants sensors to detect volcanic eruptions.

Crash Dive. Tyrone Power, Dana Andrews, and Anne Baxter in a love triangle.

Das Boot. A realistic portrayal of German submariners in World War II.

The Deep Six. Quaker Alan Ladd is drafted into the submarine service and becomes a reluctant hero.

Destination Tokyo. Captain Cary Grant's crew includes John Garfield, Dane Clark, and Alan Hale.

Ice Station Zebra. Captain Rock Hudson races a Russian submarine to the North Pole to recover military secrets.

Operation Disaster. John Mills and Richard Attenborough are caught in a trapped British submarine.

Operation Petticoat. A group of nurses are rescued by Cary Grant's submarine.

Run Silent, Run Deep. Officers Clark Gable and Burt Lancaster patch up their differences on a patrol to Tokyo Bay.

The Silent Enemy. Laurence Harvey is a British frogman working in the Mediterranean.

Submarine Command. William Holden is a heroic submarine commander.

Submarine Patrol. Richard Green and Preston Foster vie for the affections of Nancy Kelly.

Thunderball. Sean Connery alias James Bond performs heroically under the sea.

Torpedo Run. Glenn Ford sinks a Japanese carrier in Tokyo Bay.

Twenty Thousand Leagues Under the Sea. James Mason is Captain Nemo in Jules Verne's classic.

Voyage to the Bottom of the Sea. Captain Walter Pidgeon investigates a mysterious belt of radiation in the depths.

We Dive at Dawn. John Mills is a brave British captain in the Atlantic.

The Yellow Submarine. The Beatles dive in an animated musical voyage.

You Only Live Twice. A submarine figures in the antics of a James Bond–Sean Connery thriller.

CHAPTER 3

"Assassination at the bottom of the sea"

Since the dawn of time, man apparently has dreamt of exploring the ocean depths. Voyages to wondrous underwater kingdoms are a recurring mythological theme. Herodotus, Aristotle, and Pliny the Elder all wrote about attempts to build various sorts of submersible vessels.

Alexander the Great may have been the first submariner, some 333 years before the birth of Christ. Numerous early histories describe him submerging in some sort of glass barrel and seeing sea monsters and other fantastic sights. *Alexandre le Grand au Moyen-Age,* an ancient French treatise, notes, "He entered into a glass case covered with asses' skins, that had a door that could be made fast closed with chains and a ring. Upon descending he took with him such food as was necessary, and two friends for company."

A millennium and a half after Alexander, *Salman and Morolf,* a German poem circa 1200, sings of a diving boat built of leather with a long tube supplying air used to slip beneath enemy ships. The thirteenth-century scientist Roger Bacon wrote of an amazing "warlike machine . . . which being almost wholly submerged, would run through the water." Leonardo da Vinci, credited with inventing the airplane, the tank, and other devices of war, claimed to have created a submarine as well, but he deliberately left no description or sketches,

A woodcut from the 1448 *Legends of King Alexander* shows Alexander the Great being lowered into the ocean in a primitive diving bell. Alexander is believed to be the first to use such a device.

explaining, "I do not publish or divulge on account of the evil nature of men who practice assassination at the bottom of the sea."

Mother Shipton, the famous English prophetess, foresaw the modern submarine: "Under water men shall walk, shall ride, shall sleep, shall talk."

Sir Francis Bacon (1561–1626) reported, "We have heard it said that they have invented another machine, like a little ship, by the aid of which man can travel below the water for a considerable distance." No corroborating evidence survives, however.

Tales of early submarines abound, but the first detailed description appeared in a 1578 treatise, *Inventions and Devices,* written by an Englishman, William Bourne: "It is possible to make a shippe or boate that may goe under the water unto the bottome, and so come up again at your pleasure."

Bourne's plan called for a boat-shaped wooden hull, decked over and sealed watertight. Leather bags built into the bilges acted as ballast tanks, admitting seawater through holes in the hull. As the bags filled, the vessel submerged. By squeezing the water out of the bags, the operator resurfaced. A hollow mast provided fresh air. There was no indication how the boat was propelled, but Bourne solved the basic problem of a submarine: the control of buoyancy. And he sensed the shape of things to come, promoting his book as "very necessary for all generals and captains, or leaders of men as well by sea or by land."

The first man to build a workable submarine was Cornelius Van Drebbel, a Dutch physician. He amazed London in 1620 by submerging to a depth of twelve feet in his oar-powered boat and rowing across the Thames. But Van Drebbel apparently was unaware of Bourne's design. There was no way to control the buoyancy of Van Drebbel's vessel, and it took constant hard rowing to keep it submerged. He did interest James VI in his submarine, reportedly taking the monarch for a test drive.

Neither Bourne nor Van Drebbel specified what purpose their submarines would serve. In 1653 a submarine specifically planned for warfare was built at Rotterdam by a Monsieur de Son, who had a childlike faith in his creation. He boasted that it "doeth undertake in one day to destroy an hundred ships," further claiming that his boat would have the speed of a bird and be immune to fire, storm and bullets, "unless it please God." The vessel was a seventy-two-foot catamaran with a clockwork engine that proved inadequate for its task. Problems of propulsion would plague submarine designers for centuries.

There are numerous reports of crude submarines being built in the next century but little hard evidence. For example, Peter the Great of Russia ordered a submarine to be built. It was launched in 1729, during the reign of his son, Peter II, but nothing else is known.

The first recorded submarine fatality occurred on June 20, 1774. John Day, an English ship's carpenter, converted a sloop to a makeshift submarine by incorporating an air chamber and waterproofing. Day used large boulders hung from external ring bolts as detachable ballast. On his second dive something went wrong and the vessel sank in Plymouth Sound. An eyewitness report said, "She sank and Mr. Day descended with her into perpetual night."

French inventor De Son's submarine was built in Rotterdam in 1653 but was never tested. De Son immodestly promised it would "run as swift as a bird can fly" and "in one day destroy a hundred ships."

At the start of the American Revolution, David Bushnell, a brilliant young Yale graduate, felt that a submarine might be able to help break the British naval blockade of New York City. He built a submarine, the *Turtle,* which looked like an enormous pineapple grenade. It had refinements that wouldn't be seen on a submarine again for many decades—a snorkel breathing apparatus, a depth gauge, and a detachable explosive charge with a time fuse.

Bushnell put the *Turtle* through a series of tests. Everything seemed satisfactory, but the operator, Bushnell's brother, became ill after submerging for some time. No connection was made between his malady and his prolonged submersion. Bushnell needed to find and train another operator. The Continental Army provided three volunteers, and one of them, Ezra Lee, is credited with carrying out the first submarine war mission in history.

It came as night fell on September 6, 1776. Two rowboats towed Lee and the *Turtle* down the Hudson River. Near where the British squadron was anchored off Governor's Island, the boats slipped their tow and the current carried the little submarine down the river. Suddenly Lee saw he was drifting past the enemy fleet, and it took him two hours to work back upstream. Lee submerged under the hull of the British flagship, the sixty-four-gun *Eagle,* but repeatedly failed to attach the explosive charge to her copper-plated hull. He gave up when the sky started to lighten and headed upstream, the tide now in his favor. A British guard boat spotted him and gave chase. Lee set the time fuse and cut loose the explosive charge. The blast distracted the British boat, allowing the *Turtle* to float down the river to safety. The British fleet scattered. The primitive submarine had given the British something to think about.

The *Turtle* is believed to have made two other unsuccessful attacks on British ships. After the war she was being transported aboard a ship which ran aground on a reef and was lost to the sea. Bushnell's submarine received a fitting epitaph. In a letter to Thomas Jefferson, George Washington described the boat as an "effort of genius." But the government wasn't interested in buying Bushnell's submarine. Another 120 years would pass before the American Navy would take the submarine seriously.

A similar submarine reportedly was in operation during the War of 1812. The seventy-four-gun British ship *Ramillies* reported in July 1813 that she was attacked by a "diving boat" which penetrated the copper sheathing on her bottom, but apparently was unable to attach an explosive charge.

Robert Fulton, the Yankee inventor, was interested in submarines. An ardent pacifist, he saw the submarine as a way to destroy navies and rid the world of repressive armaments. After producing a workable design, Fulton sailed to France. He believed the French Revolution was a great force for freedom, and he wanted to place his submarine in its service.

On December 13, 1797, he approached the Directory, the commit-

A modern drawing shows that Bushnell's *Turtle* had vertical and horizontal propellers, pumps to fill and empty the ballast tanks, a torpedo screw, ventilators, and even a primitive depth gauge.

During the American Revolution, David Bushnell attacked British ships blockading New York harbor in his *Turtle,* attaching explosive devices to their hulls with a bit-stock type tool.

Robert Fulton tried to sell his submarine *Nautilus,* shown sailing on the surface and submerged, to Napoleon to use against the British, then to the British to use against Napoleon.

tee that ruled France, offering a "mechanical engine" to destroy the British Navy then blockading the French coast. Fulton proposed building the submarine at his own expense; for every British ship it sank he would be paid four thousand francs per gun. The nearly bankrupt Directory decided that if the submarine sank even one British warship the Directory would sink, too.

The Directory negotiated the price down but refused to grant naval status to the submarine crew; if captured they could be hanged as pirates. Discouraged, Fulton tried unsuccessfully to find Dutch backing. Two years later he was back in France, negotiating with Napoleon Bonaparte. The British still blockaded France, and Napoleon welcomed the idea of a new weapon. He gave Fulton ten thousand francs to build the submarine.

The submarine, christened the *Nautilus,* was launched in 1801. Cylindrical in shape, it had a copper hull covering iron frames, a conning tower, and diving planes. Propelled by a hand-operated screw, the *Nautilus* used a kite-shaped sail while on the surface. On the Seine opposite the Hôtel des Invalides, the submarine descended to twenty-five feet.

Sea trials were scheduled off the port of Brest, but the Maritime Prefect of Brest decided he could not sanction trials for what he regarded as an inhumane instrument of war. The situation disintegrated into arguments over money, denouncements of Fulton as a charlatan, and French admirals publicly calling the submarine an unsound idea. More to the point, a cease-fire was being negotiated with Britain, and a submarine could only complicate matters. Napoleon withdrew his support.

In 1804 Fulton went to England and was received by Prime Minister William Pitt, who appointed a committee to investigate whether Britain should purchase the American's submarine. In a demonstration, Fulton blew up a Navy brig. The Royal Navy's response was a classic example of what happens when a conservative establishment is presented with a challenging idea. Pitt was called "the greatest fool that ever existed to encourage a mode of warfare which those who commanded the sea did not want, and which, if successful, would deprive them of it." Fulton abandoned the submarine for the steamboat.

An English smuggler and adventurer named Captain Johnson reportedly built a submarine in 1820 to rescue Napoleon from his St. Helena imprisonment for a reward of 40,000 pounds sterling. Napoleon died before the submarine was ready. Johnson then tried to get France to purchase five submarines, but nothing came of it.

War broke out between Denmark and Prussia in 1850, and the Danish fleet blockaded the Prussian coast. Wilhelm Bauer, a Bavarian artillery sergeant, designed a submarine, the *Brandtaucher* (Fire Diver), a sheet-iron rectangular tank propelled by a hand wheel. Water ballast lowered buoyancy, and the diving angle was changed by moving a heavy weight back and forth inside the submarine. The hull tended to develop leaks when submerged.

The maiden voyage was a success, and the Danes withdrew their ships from Kiel. But a month later, diving in fifty feet of water in Kiel Harbor, the submarine's stern plating collapsed. Bauer coolly told his two crewmen to let the boat flood so that air pressure would force open the hatches. Five hours later they reached the surface, the first to escape a damaged submarine.

Bauer went to Britain during the Crimean War to sell a submarine. There were talks of "Lord Palmerston's submarine," but all that is known is that Scott Russell, a well-known British naval architect, produced a design for a submarine after several meetings with Bauer, and that Prime Minister Henry Palmerston approved funding a prototype. Apparently it was never built.

Bauer went to Russia in 1855 with a commission to build a 52-foot submarine called *Seeteufel* (Sea Devil). During the coronation ceremonies of Tsar Alexander II, the submarine submerged with musicians aboard. They struck up the Russian national anthem and it was heard faintly by the guests ashore—a demonstration of how well and how far sound travels underwater.

French interest revived, and in 1858 the Minister of Marine invited proposals for a submarine to protect the coast. Charles Brun was given a contract and built the 140-foot *Plongeur*. It incorporated a number of innovations, including reservoirs for compressed air that both expelled water from the ballast tanks and drove a four-cylinder engine.

What was lacking now was a proper submarine weapon. The *Plongeur* carried a spar torpedo, a canister of explosive on the end of a

After Greece bought a Garrett and Nordenfeldt submarine, her traditional enemy, Turkey, bought two. One of them is shown here on display at a Constantinople dock and submerging amid curious boaters.

pole which was detonated by poking it against the side of an enemy ship. It would prove to be counterproductive.

In the American Civil War, the Confederacy built small vessels called "Davids" to attack the Goliath-like Union warships blockading southern ports. Davids were torpedo boats that traveled very low in the water, submerging for brief periods with only the superstructure visible above the water.

The first David was swamped by the wake of a passing steamer but was raised and put back in action. Off Charleston, South Carolina, on October 5, 1863, she rammed her spar torpedo into the Union ironclad *New Ironsides,* causing extensive damage but killing most of the David's crew.

Another submarine, the *H. L. Hunley,* named after her designer, was built of steel boilerplate and resembled a cigar. It was 40 feet long and only 42 inches in diameter, and the crew came aboard through hatches at either end. The *Hunley* also was easily swamped, sinking three times in sea trials with a loss of twenty-three crewmen.

On the night of February 17, 1864, the *Hunley,* commanded by Lieutenant George E. Dixon and carrying a crew of eight, crossed Charleston Harbor under cover of darkness. Spotting the Union fleet, Dixon chose the new 1,264-ton *Housatonic* as his target.

The deck officer on the *Housatonic* caught sight of the *Hunley,* but before the ship could get under way the submarine was alongside. The 30-foot projecting spar, supporting the canister of gunpowder, exploded on contact with the frigate, just forward of the main mast on the starboard side, abreast of the magazine. The *Housatonic* lifted bodily out of the water, then settled rapidly by the stern, the first ship ever sunk by a submarine.

Sunk, too, was the *Hunley* with all hands. She simply disappeared. It is believed that if there had been some way to detonate the spar torpedo from inside with the hatch sealed, she might have survived.

Early in the war, another Confederate submarine turned up in Philadelphia. Harbor police stumbled on a "submarine monster" tied up at an island in the Delaware River. According to Robert F. Burgess's *Ships Beneath the Sea: A History of Subs and Submersibles,* the *Philadelphia Evening Bulletin* on May 17, 1861, reported:

> Never since the first flush of the bombardment of Fort Sumter, has there been an excitement in the city equal to that which was caused . . . by the capture of a mysterious vessel which was said to be an infernal machine, which was to be used for all sorts of treasonable purposes, including the trifling pastime of scuttling and blowing up government men-of-war. For a few days past the police have had their attention directed to the movements, not of a "long, low, black schooner", but of an iron submarine boat, to which very extraordinary abilities and infernal propensities were attributed.

The owner was Brutus de Villeroi, a Frenchman who had been trying to sell the submarine to the Union Navy. The seizure was a publicity break. The commandant of the Philadelphia Navy Yard examined the submarine and was impressed. A few months later de Villeroi wrote to President Lincoln to press his case. His letter concluded, "With a few such boats maneuvered each one by about a dozen men and the most formidable fleet can be annihilated in a short time."

De Villeroi was awarded a contract, and his *Alligator* was launched April 30, 1862. It saw no action, although some experts believed that it could have "destroyed, or at least rendered harmless" the Confederate ironclad *Merrimack* at Hampton Roads. The *Alligator* sank while under tow off Cape Hatteras on April 2, 1863.

Another Union submarine, nicknamed the *Intelligent Whale,* also was star-crossed. Thirty-nine men drowned during sea trials. Designed by Oliver Halstead, the boat apparently had promise, except for the

The U.S. Navy in 1873 bought the 26-foot, hand-powered *Intelligent Whale,* designed by Oliver Halstead. It was a total failure and soured the Navy on submarines for a number of years.

all too common tendency to be easily swamped.

The periscope was developed during the Civil War, but for iron-clads, not submarines. The *Monitor Osage* used a periscope to locate a Confederate cavalry unit taking cover on the high banks of the Red River in Arkansas.

In 1866 an Englishman, Robert Whitehead, invented the self-pro-pelled torpedo (the word *torpedo* comes from the Latin for electric eel, *Torpedo Electruicus*). The Whitehead torpedo was used on surface ships for decades before a submarine capable of using it would be developed.

The man who almost singlehandedly created the modern subma-rine was a stubborn, idiosyncratic man who dreamed of freeing his native Ireland from British rule. He was born John Phillip Holland on February 24, 1841, in Liscannor on the Irish coast, and as a boy he was plagued with ill health. At seventeen, he took the vows of the teaching order of the Irish Christian Brothers. He soon found another passion, the Irish Revolutionary Brotherhood, dedicated to the cause of Irish freedom. Swept up in clandestine activities, he continued to teach because he needed the money.

Holland had a restless, curious mind and a knack for science. He decided that a submarine might attack the British fleet and tip the balance of power in Ireland's favor. He designed a submarine, but couldn't get it built. In 1873 he sailed for Boston to join his family.

No one in America was interested in his submarine, and he resumed teaching in Paterson, New Jersey, while refining his design. He wanted to work with other submarine designers but couldn't. According to Richard K. Morris's *John P. Holland, 1841–1914,* Holland later wrote:

> . . . the development of vessels of this type was hindered by the secrecy main-tained by everyone who had any knowledge of their design. Governments guarded the particulars of their experiments in order to preserve for themselves the advantage conferred by a successful submarine boat, and the results of individ-ual efforts were just as carefully hidden to prevent the competition of other inventors. As each designer was thus compelled to face the problem without the knowledge of what had been accomplished by his predecessors, he had to dis-cover for himself the main requirements of a submarine vessel, and to foresee and provide against difficulties.

But working alone might have been an advantage. Holland was free of the mistakes of the past.

The Fenian Brotherhood, a large, fiercely militant force for Irish freedom, became enchanted with Holland, and its newspaper *Irish World* launched an appeal for funds to build his submarine. Money poured in from the Irish-American community. Prospective backers gathered at Coney Island to watch Holland demonstrate a thirty-inch model of his submarine; they liked what they saw and opened their purses. The Albany Iron Works in Paterson built Holland's subma-rine: a lozenge-shaped craft, 14½ feet long and 2½ feet high, weigh-ing 2¼ tons, and costing $4,000.

The submarine was taken to the edge of the Passaic River. Report-edly someone on a nearby bridge looked down and said, "I see the

As a young man in Ireland, John Holland envisioned submarines freeing his country from England by destroying the British fleet. His first design in 1878 looked more like an alien spacecraft than a submarine.

Professor has built a coffin for himself." In the water the submarine settled rapidly and sank. Holland had miscalculated. The boat was designed for salt water; the Passaic River was fresh water, making a critical difference in buoyancy.

Adjustments were made within the hour and the boat floated properly, but now the two-cylinder gas engine wouldn't start. Holland spent weeks adapting the engine to steam. A launch generated steam and passed it through a rubber hose to the submarine's engine.

The launch, carrying a group of influential Fenians, chugged off down the river to an area free of other craft. Holland was in a space forty-six inches long and about twenty-four inches high with his head poking up into a sealed conning tower. He flooded the two ballast tanks and pushed the lever that controlled the diving rudders. Small tanks forward and aft were left empty to provide a slight positive buoyancy to bring the craft to the surface in an emergency. The submarine submerged to a depth of twelve feet, reappearing safely a short distance away. Later Holland stayed submerged for an hour.

The trial runs demonstrated Holland's grasp of the principles of buoyancy and stability. Working alone, he had surpassed the work of earlier submarine designers. The Fenians agreed to fund another "wrecking boat." Holland turned his full attention to submarine design.

In 1879 the Fenians put up $23,000 for another submarine, the *Fenian Ram,* 31 feet long, 6 feet wide, and propelled by a gasoline engine. A freak accident during sea trials foundered the *Fenian Ram,* and it cost the backers $3,000 to have the boat raised. The trials dragged on, and the backers ran out of patience. They broke into the shipyard and towed the submarine away. They attempted to use the *Fenian Ram* themselves, finally giving up. Holland now had lost interest. "I'll let her rot on their hands," he said. The *Fenian Ram* was never in the water again.

Near bankruptcy, Holland tried to sell a submarine to the Navy Department. To make ends meet, he took a job as a draftsman at the Pneumatic Gun Company, where he met Captain Edmund L. Zalinski, an Army ordnance expert. The captain had a new "dynamite gun"

"Noname's" Latest and Best Stories are Published in This Library

FRANK READE LIBRARY

Entered as Second Class Matter at the New York, N. Y., Post Office, October 5, 1892.

No. 112. {COMPLETE} FRANK TOUSEY, PUBLISHER, 31 & 36 NORTH MOORE STREET, NEW YORK, {PRICE} Vol. V.
New York, July 26, 1895. {ISSUED WEEKLY.} {5 CENTS.}

Entered according to the Act of Congress, in the year 1895, by FRANK TOUSEY, in the office of the Librarian of Congress, at Washington, D. C.

THE UNDERGROUND SEA; or, Frank Reade, Jr.'s Subterranean Cruise in His Submarine Boat.

By "NONAME."

Quick as a flash the young inventor acted. He rushed forward, and with his hatchet dealt the creature a blow just back of the head. It was well directed and given with great force.

At the turn of the century, boys were fascinated with submarines, and pulp magazines fed them a fanciful diet of underwater adventures. Note the three-decker submarine in the background.

and thought it should be mounted on a submarine. He could only afford a wooden submarine, however, and Holland reluctantly agreed to build it. Launched in 1885, it was an absolute failure. Holland later complained that the Zalinski boat set his career back ten years. Whatever the reason, Holland disappeared from the scene for more than a decade. Meanwhile submarine history was being made by, of all people, an English curate.

CHAPTER
4
"There, sir! That is the perfection of vessels!"

George William Garrett, the son of a Manchester, England, vicar, was admitted to Trinity College in Dublin at seventeen, and passed all the first-year examinations in his first week. Science was his first love, and after graduation he was appointed an assistant master at the Manchester Mechanics Institute. There he earned certificates in science, art, physical geography, geology, mathematics, and higher chemistry. To placate his father, Garrett also studied theology, and in 1873 he was ordained as curate. His primary interest, though, was submarine design.

After Garrett returned from a voyage around the world in 1877, the Russo-Turkish War broke out. He was intrigued when Russian torpedo boats were thwarted by Turkish harbor-defense nets. He felt that a submarine could have gone under the nets.

Garrett invented a self-contained breathing suit, the forerunner of today's scuba. Demonstrating it for the French Ministry of Marine, he stayed below the surface of the Seine for thirty-seven minutes, but the French weren't interested in breathing suits. They wanted submarines.

In 1878 Garrett was awarded a patent for "Improvements in and Appertaining to Submarine or Subaqueous Boats or Vessels for

George W. Garrett's 1879 *Resurgam* was steam-powered. A head of steam was raised, the fire put out, and the heat in the tanks generated enough steam to run the submarine ten miles underwater.

Removing, Destroying, Laying or Placing Torpedoes in Channels and other Situations, and for other Purposes." He founded his own firm that year, the Garrett Submarine Navigation and Pneumataphore Company, Ltd., financed by his father and some Manchester businessmen.

He built an experimental submarine, 14 feet long and 5 feet in diameter. Instead of diving rudders for trimming the boat, Garrett borrowed an idea of William Bourne's: a piston inside the boat which altered the boat's volume by drawing in or expelling water. A hand crank powered the boat. Gauntlets of greased leather installed in the hull enabled the pilot to reach outside and attach an explosive charge to a ship. Garrett christened his first submarine *Resurgam*, Latin for "I will rise again."

The submarine was criticized in the press and from the pulpit as an immoral weapon. In the prospectus for his company Garrett wrote, "As to the inventions being for murdering people—this is all nonsense. Every contribution made by science to improve instruments of war makes war shorter and, in the end, less terrible to human progress."

Resurgam performed well in sea trials, and Garrett built a larger boat and powered it with steam. It was cigar-shaped, weighing close to 30 tons, and the hull could withstand pressure at a depth of nearly 150 feet. The submarine made two to three knots and could stay submerged for as long as steam could be produced. If the air inside the boat ran out, the crew could use Garrett's underwater breathing suit.

Resurgam II was launched on December 10, 1879, at Birkenhead. Garrett and a crew of two took the submarine down the Mersey River under her own power. Garrett planned to steam to Portsmouth to show his submarine to the wealthy Swedish arms manufacturer Thorsten Nordenfeldt. He purchased a small steam yacht, the *Elfin,* to tow the boat and serve as her escort.

As they headed west along the Welsh coast, a storm rose quickly and the towing hawser parted. Garrett watched *Resurgam II* flounder and sink, never to be recovered.

Garrett was in financial trouble, and Nordenfelt seemed his only hope. They formed a partnership: Garrett had the submarine patent, Nordenfeldt the money. They built a submarine at Stockholm, the *Nordenfeldt No. 1,* and sold it to Greece in 1883. Three years later Turkey bought two submarines of the same design. The submarines had problems—the boiler often leaked carbon monoxide into the boat, and the ballast tanks made it rock—but they were the first submarines to use the Whitehead automatic torpedo, which fired at a safe distance from the target.

Nordenfelt and Garrett built three more submarines. One participated in the Golden Jubilee Review of the British Navy in 1887, attracting the attention of the visiting tsar, who purchased it. But the submarine was damaged on the way to Russia, and the tsar refused to honor the contract. The other two submarines went unsold.

The partnership was dissolved. Nordenfelt designed a new submarine which no one wanted to buy, so he went back to selling machine guns. Garrett emigrated to the United States and served as an Army engineer in the Spanish-American War. In 1902, nearly destitute, he died in New York at the age of fifty.

A Garrett and Nordenfeldt submarine had a dinghy and a smokestack but no periscope. After selling only a few Garrett boats, Nordenfeldt gave up and went back to the machine gun business.

The major problem of submarines in those years was propulsion. Neither steam nor the gasoline engine proved satisfactory. Four designers in four countries worked independently on what would be the answer: electric-powered submarines.

In New York, Josiah Tuck in 1884 built a 30-foot, electric-powered submarine called the *Peace Maker,* tested it successfully, but couldn't find a buyer. In England, J. F. Waddington, a shipbuilder, designed a 37-foot boat in 1885 called the *Porpoise* and equipped it with a powerful electric motor which enabled it to cruise 150 miles. The *Porpoise* boasted two other significant innovations: hull planes that automatically kept it horizontal when submerged, and two Whitehead torpedoes for armament. Also in 1885, M. Goubet received a French patent for a submarine design incorporating an electric motor. The *Goubet I* had a 16-foot hull made of bronze and cast as a single piece. The two-man crew sat back to back, looking out of windows in a small conning tower.

A young Spanish naval officer, Isaac Peral, came up with the same answer to the propulsion problem. His 1886 design included an electric motor powered by accumulator batteries. The Spanish Navy built the submarine, and it caught the attention of the French. The leading French naval architect, Dupuy de Lome, began designing a submarine incorporating Peral's idea; his associate, Gustave Zede, completed it after de Lome's death.

The *Gymnote,* French for eel, was built in 1887, 60 feet long with a hull diameter of 5 feet 10 inches, a Whitehead torpedo mounted in her bow, and an electric motor. The French rebuilt it several times to test new ideas. In 1896 a French competition drew some thirty designs for a 200-ton submarine with a surface range of one hundred miles. The winner was Maxime Laubeuf, and his design was the link between the early prototypes and the submarines of World War I.

Laubeuf's *Narval* used two propulsion systems: an electric motor for running submerged and steam for the surface. More important, the steam engine could recharge the accumulator batteries. It had a double hull in which fuel and water ballast could be stored, an innovation still in use today. The principal drawback was that it took the *Narval* twenty minutes to submerge, but the French Navy liked her well enough to order four more.

In America, John Holland followed reports of the progress of the French boats and grudgingly admitted that they had merit. "Totally sick and disgusted" with the U.S. Navy's lack of interest in his designs, he decided that some publicity might help. He published an article entitled "Can New York be Bombarded?" describing the weaknesses of America's fleet and its coastal defenses, and how a few submarines could correct them.

The Navy took notice of the article and announced an open competition for a "submarine torpedo-boat." No designer met the specifications: fifteen knots on the surface, eight submerged—a performance level not attained until the late 1930s. Another competition was held

with more realistic specifications. Holland won, but the Navy decided
not to build his boat.

If the Navy wasn't fascinated with submarines, the public certainly
was. Jules Verne's epic science-fiction fantasy *Twenty Thousand
Leagues Under the Sea* was an international sensation in 1869.
Designers worked feverishly to create their own version of a *Nautilus,* but most met with varying degrees of failure.

Many of the designs were bizarre: a two-part submarine, the
underwater part with two columns supporting an above-water platform; a submarine resembling a corkscrew, which the designer claimed

Jules Verne's fantasy submarine
Nautilus. His 1870 book *20,000
Leagues Under the Sea,* a
worldwide success, captured
the imagination of young Simon
Lake, inspiring him to design
and build submarines.

would enable her to twist through the water so swiftly it could cross the Atlantic in twenty-eight hours; one with pointed ends that theoretically could be dropped off while submerged, enabling the center section to float to the surface; another featured hand-turned paddles and a rubber-band motor; a German design for a submarine shaped like "an ovoid bent askew" with a large picture window.

Germany had the most workable submarines, adaptations of Garrett and Nordenfelt's design. They were large, more than one hundred feet in length, and attracted worldwide attention in the kaiser's 1890 fleet maneuvers.

Still in eclipse and broke, Holland took a menial job in a dredging company paying four dollars a day. In his spare time, he developed an idea for an airplane that could take off vertically. Nothing came of it, but it caught the attention of influential people. His luck began to change in 1893 when Grover Cleveland, a proponent of the submarine, regained the presidency.

Another submarine design competition was held. Holland won, and the Navy awarded him $200,000 to produce his design. The John P. Holland Torpedo Boat Company was formed, and a Baltimore shipyard was contracted to build the submarine, the *Plunger*. Contract specifications forced design concessions on Holland. The *Plunger*, launched in 1897, was so disappointing that her sea trials were called off. Holland then convinced the Navy to allow him to build a second submarine of his own design, and immediately started to construct his personal vision of a submarine.

The second submarine, *Holland VI*, launched the following year, was the forerunner of all modern submarines. It was 53 feet 10 inches

John P. Holland emerges from the conning tower of the U.S.S. *Holland,* the first submarine purchased by the Navy. The genius of this Irish-American led to the development of the modern submarine.

The Navy forced its design ideas on Holland and the *Plunger* was the result, a technical and financial failure. Holland saved the day by building a submarine of his own design that proved to be a success.

There, sir! That is the perfection of vessels!

Holland's torpedo boat company was short-lived. To build a submarine of his own design he borrowed heavily and lost financial control to the supplier of storage batteries. He died an old and bitter man.

An 1898 drawing of a Holland "torpedo" boat took many liberties. On the surface his boat was powered by a gas engine, she was submerged by batteries, and she fired torpedoes, not cannons.

long with a diameter of 10 feet 3 inches, displaced 74 tons submerged, with plating over a frame skeleton. A 45-horsepower gasoline engine gave it a speed of eight knots on the surface and also charged the accumulator batteries. A 50-horsepower motor provided nearly the same speed underwater. The *Holland VI* had one tube and carried three Whitehead torpedoes and a new compensating system for maintaining the trim when a torpedo was fired. A system of clutches allowed the engine to charge the batteries while either running or standing—an innovation that would be used on submarines for more than fifty years.

Alan H. Burgoyne, a contemporary British authority, wrote, "Of this vessel perhaps more has been heard than of any other ship or boat in the world. She is the prototype of the latest submarine ordered by Great Britain and the American government and is also, without doubt, the commencement of the 'really successful' submarine."

The submarine performed well on sea trials. On St. Patrick's Day 1898 it made a dive off Staten Island. Several days later the United States declared war on Spain. Assistant Secretary of the Navy Theodore Roosevelt, who monitored the submarine's sea trials, wrote Navy Secretary John D. Long, "I think that the Holland submarine boat should be purchased. Evidently she has great possibilities in her for harbor defense. Sometimes she doesn't work perfectly, but often does, and I don't think in the present emergency we can afford to let her slip."

Holland offered to take his submarine to Havana and blow up the Spanish fleet, but the Navy demurred. Building the submarine had

A naval officer poses with the civilian crew of a Holland submarine during sea trials. The Navy, dominated by battleship admirals, resisted adopting new ideas, whether submarines or airplanes.

stretched the resources of the Holland Boat Company to the breaking
point. The company that supplied the batteries for the *Holland VI*
stepped in and drove a hard bargain. The Holland Boat Company
became The Electric Boat Company, and John Holland was no longer
in financial control.

On April 11, 1900, the Navy finally accepted the *Holland VI.* The
next year Holland built a larger boat, the *Fulton,* but the Navy didn't
buy it and he sold it to Russia. Five Holland submarines were sold to
Japan, although they apparently weren't used in the Russo-Japanese
War of 1904–1905.

The U.S. Navy bestirred itself in 1903 and ordered six new Holland
submarines—the *Adder, Grampus, Moccasin, Porpoise, Pike,* and
Shark. These submarines formed the first United States Submarine
Service. Other countries began buying submarines from Holland.
Britain, though still committed to ruling the sea with surface ships,
ordered five in response to France's submarine acquisitions.

Holland surpassed his *Holland VI* in 1906, building the 105-foot,
270-ton *Octopus.* The new boat carried a crew of fifteen and could
make eleven knots on the surface, ten submerged. *Octopus* astounded
observers by test-diving to a depth of 205 feet. The Navy was impressed
but demanded that he test the *Octopus* against a new submarine, the
Simon Lake X, named for Holland's closest competitor, a peppery young
redhead who also knew the frustration of trying to sell to the Navy.
The performance duel lasted ten days and received considerable
attention in the press. The *Octopus* nosed out Lake's boat and was
purchased.

The career of Simon Lake mirrored Holland's trials and tribula-
tions. When he was eleven, Lake read of Captain Nemo and his submarine *Nautilus* in *Twenty Thousand Leagues Under the Sea,* and
his life was changed forever. He reread the book countless times, and
loved to quote from it, regaling his young friends with such passages
as:

> No defects to be afraid of, for the double shell is as firm as iron; no rigging to
> attend to; no sails for the wind to carry away; no boilers to burst; no fire to fear,
> for the vessel is made of iron, not of wood; no coal to run short, for electricity is
> the only mechanical agent; no collision to fear, for it alone swims in deep water;
> no tempest to brave, for when it dives below the water it reaches absolute tran-
> quillity. There, sir! that is the perfection of vessels!

Lake grew to know Verne's *Nautilus* so well that he started to
imagine improvements. He took a new interest in his school work,
and rose to the head of the class. He found that he had a flair for
science, and he was determined to build a submarine someday. Two
years out of school he patented a steering gear for high-wheeled bicy-
cles, then a winding gear for oystermen, and a capping device for the
canning industry, all the while working on designs for a submarine
he called the *Argonaut.*

Learning of a Navy competition for submarine designs, Lake, then twenty-seven, went to Washington in 1893. His competitors were George Baker of Chicago and John Philip Holland. Lake lost and barely had enough money left to get home to Atlantic Heights, New Jersey. But the experience left him more determined to build his submarine.

Failing to raise money, Lake planned a smaller boat, the *Argonaut Junior,* and members of his family put up the money to build it. When completed, the 14-foot submarine bore an uncanny resemblance to an old-time flatiron. The hull had flat sides; the conning tower was amidships, a wooden box with portholes. A unique feature was an air lock pressurized by compressed air to permit a diver to leave and reenter. *Argonaut Junior* also had two wheels forward mounted on an axle, and a third smaller wheel at the stern. Despite its odd appearance, the boat performed well. Lake formed the Lake Submarine Company, capitalized at $2,500.

By selling shares, Lake was able to build the submarine he had originally planned. By coincidence, his *Argonaut I* was built in the same shipyard as the *Plunger,* and while the *Plunger* was a failure, Lake's boat did well in her sea trials. Lake took his boat to New York and invited newspaper reporters to take a cruise. The publicity stunt got a big play in the press, but proved of no help in attracting either buyers or more investors.

Seeking further publicity, Lake made a two-thousand-mile tour of Chesapeake Bay, submerging as often as possible. It was the longest voyage of a submarine to date, and the first extended observation of marine life ever made.

On February 15, 1898, the battleship *Maine* was sunk in Havana, and Lake, like Holland, offered his submarine to the Navy, but was turned down. Lake saw another opportunity later that year when the Navy laid a mine field across Hampton Roads, a channel connecting the James and Elizabeth rivers with Chesapeake Bay, apparently anticipating the Spanish fleet. Lake took the *Argonaut* under the mine field, carefully noting through a porthole how the mine field was laid out. He wrote the Navy about his escapade, including the details of the mine field, and pointed out that his submarine was capable of both laying and disarming mines. The Navy did not respond.

While returning to New Jersey, the submarine was caught in a severe sleet storm with towering waves. Lake lashed himself into the conning tower and shouted directions to his two crewmen below. The *Argonaut* made it, although more than a hundred ships were lost. Newspapers around the world reported the submarine's performance. Even Jules Verne cabled congratulations. Lake always regarded this as one of the high points of his life.

Lake raised enough money to build a more conventional submarine—no wheels, no flat-sided hull, no portholes. Built in 1902, the *Protector* was a 65-foot, 130-ton boat with a twin propulsion system similar to Holland's. *Protector* was the first submarine to mount a gun on its foredeck, and to have a workable periscope, which Lake called an "omniscope."

A demonstration for the Navy aroused no interest, but the Army was impressed and ordered five. The Navy successfully lobbied to get the appropriation bill defeated, though, and Lake began looking to other countries for possible sales. Russia, at war with Japan, agreed to buy the *Protector* and five more of the same design. Lake and his crew went to Russia to show the tsar's Navy how to operate the boat.

No submarines saw action in the Russo-Japanese War, but Russia was enchanted with them and wanted to expand its underwater fleet. Lake built two submarines for Austria, then set up a joint operation with the Krupp armament makers in Germany. He neglected to protect his patents in Germany, however, and received no royalties.

Lake returned home and built the *Simon Lake X,* incorporating all he had learned from the *Argonaut* series and the *Protector*. The Navy turned it down after it was tested against Holland's *Octopus.* An angry Lake sold the boat to his old customer, Russia. Later, Congress took over the purchasing of submarines and commissioned Lake to build a submarine. However, the Navy's requirements were formidable:

> The Lake Company will build at its own expense a submarine which will be:
> Faster on the surface or under it than any boat now building, either in the United States or abroad.
> It will have a greater radius of action, more powerful armament, eight torpedo tubes, safety features by which a man can escape when the boat is submerged, and facilities for planting mines and cutting cables.
> It will do more than the United States Government has ever asked that any submarine do. If it does not do all that is claimed for it, the United States Government need never pay us a cent of money.

The large wheels on Simon Lake's *Argonaut* enabled her to crawl on the bottom of the sea. To publicize his submarine, Lake took her on a history-making 2,000-mile underwater tour of Chesapeake Bay.

In response, Lake designed and built the *Seal,* a 161-foot, 400-ton boat, the largest built up to that time. It carried a crew of twenty-four and was armed with six torpedoes. On October 12, 1912, the Navy accepted the *Seal.* Simon Lake finally achieved the recognition in his own country he had craved for so long.

The last years of John Philip Holland were unhappy. Others were reaping the profits from his superlative designs. He had a small income from early patents, but his bitterness over the loss of his company dulled his enthusiasm and ruined his health. He put aside submarines and again turned to aviation, writing a book, *How to Fly as a Bird.*

Holland died in a hospital in Newark on August 12, 1914, five days after the beginning of World War I. It probably would have pleased the old Fenian had he lived to see how submarines soon would bedevil the British.

CHAPTER 5

"Build more submarines!"

When Gavrilo Princep assassinated Archduke Francis Ferdinand of Austria on June 28, 1914, none of the great powers were putting much stock in submarines. They built them because their traditional enemies built them, but victory at sea was the business of battleships and cruisers. These ships reigned supreme, in battle and in naval appropriations.

In 1901 Admiral Alfred von Tirpitz had told the Reichstag that the German Navy didn't need submarines, explaining, "We have no money to waste on experimental vessels. We must leave such luxuries to wealthier states like France and England." But when Russia purchased three submarines, Tirpitz changed his mind. The first submarine joined the German fleet in 1908.

By 1914 Germany had twenty-nine submarines, and both Britain and France had about twice that many. The major powers built their own submarines, Britain and France from modified John Holland designs, Germany from Simon Lake's design. German submarines had the advantage of a German invention, the diesel engine. Remarkably reliable, it produced no spark, and diesel oil was not as dangerous to have aboard a submarine as gasoline. Diesel engines gave U-boats, from the German *unterseeboot,* a range of 3,000 miles, which would work to Germany's advantage. By contrast, Britain and

France developed shorter-range submarines: small, sturdy, and fast.

Despite this activity, not much thought had been given to how submarines would be used in time of war. The Hague Convention of 1899 codified the rules of civilized naval warfare, and it was assumed they applied to submarines. The rules said a warship was not to fire on an unarmed merchantman. To determine if a ship was carrying contraband, she would be ordered to stop and her papers examined. If the ship was trading with the enemy, she could be taken as a prize, or sunk after the crew were put aboard lifeboats. If the weather was bad, the crew would be taken aboard the warship.

But to stop a merchantman a submarine would have to surface, exposing herself to attack. A submarine crew was too small to spare men to oversee a prize ship. Nor was there room aboard a submarine to hold the crew of a merchantman. The Hague Convention did not address itself to these problems, perhaps assuming that submarines would concentrate on attacking warships.

The first wartime confrontation was conducted according to the Hague rules. Off the coast of Norway on October 20, 1914, the small British steamer *Glitra* was stopped by the German submarine *U-17*. The crew was put in lifeboats, the sea cocks opened, and the *Glitra* went to the bottom, the first merchantman to be sunk by a submarine. In the first six months of the war, ten merchantmen were similarly sunk by U-boats. Their captains had been cautioned not to waste torpedoes.

But the primary objective of a submarine was to sink warships, not merchantmen. Shortly after war was declared, a British submarine, the *E-9,* slipped into the bight of Helgoland north of Wilhelmshaven in the North Sea and found the German cruiser *Hela* lying at anchor. Two Whitehead torpedoes sent her to the bottom. The *Hela* was the first warship to be sunk by a submarine's torpedoes since the *Housatonic* was dispatched by a Confederate David in the Civil War.

In December 1914 another British submarine, the *B-11,* amazingly threaded its way through the Dardanelles mine fields to the Sea of Marmara, sank the Turkish battleship *Messudiyeh,* and returned home safely despite a malfunctioning compass.

The U-boats also got in some early punches. The *U-21* sank the flotilla leader H.M.S. *Pathfinder,* most of the crew going down with the ship.

Both British and German submarines experienced problems. British torpedoes ran beneath their targets; German submarines were plagued by mechanical breakdowns. The *U-15* broke down at sea, and while on the surface being repaired she was rammed and sunk by the cruiser H.M.S. *Birmingham.* Another U-boat struck a British mine and went down with all hands. Both British and German warships accidentally fired on their own submarines.

Life aboard a World War I submarine was hard, whatever flag it flew. The average submarine was about 150 feet long, carrying three officers and a crew of thirty in varying degrees of discomfort. There were bunks for only half the crew, and the men slept in shifts. No matter how exhausted, everyone turned to when the claxon sounded, for the safety of the boat was at stake.

There was no refrigeration, and after a few days at sea only canned rations could be served. There were no bathing facilities. The toilet used air pressure to flush waste out of the submarine, a tricky business. If the water pressure outside the submarine exceeded that of the air pressure inside, a phenomenon occurred called "getting your own back."

Interiors were cramped. Moving from one part of a submarine to another was arduous. The interior could be brutally hot while the submarine traveled on the surface, bitterly cold submerged.

The smell inside defied description, a noxious mixture composed of the aroma of unwashed bodies, rotting food, excreta, fumes from the bilge, and smoke from the diesel on the surface or battery fumes submerged. No wonder American submariners called them "pig boats." Only dying on a submarine was worse than living on one.

But the submariners surmounted their hardships and were surprisingly effective. On September 22, 1914, the *U-9* singlehandedly sank three cruisers, *Aboukir, Cressy,* and *Hague.* The British admiralty was shocked. An admiral said, "It is the German Fleet that now controls the North Sea!" The Grand Fleet hastily moved to the west coast of Scotland to wait until the antisubmarine defenses at its Scapa Flow base could be increased. Germany scored a strategic victory but did not exploit it.

Suddenly submarines were all the British could think about. "Build more submarines!" First Sea Lord Jackie Fisher urged Winston Churchill, first lord of the admiralty. Shipyards sharply increased the construction of Holland-type submarines.

British submarines performed admirably. Two legendary captains, Noel Laurence and Max Horton, harassed German squadrons in the Baltic. Horton torpedoed eight destroyers off the Danish coast. During a battle between German and Russian ships, he slipped in unnoticed and damaged a German battleship with a torpedo.

Meanwhile Laurence also torpedoed a battleship. He spotted the entire German battle-cruiser squadron and fired once, striking the *Moltke,* damaging her severely. He eluded the escort destroyers and escaped. After his attack, the German squadron turned back from its planned attack on Riga, Latvia.

Germany put a price on Laurence's head, and Grand Admiral Prince Heinrich announced, "I regard the destruction of a British submarine as being at least as valuable as that of a Russian armored cruiser."

Under the Anglo-French alliance, most French submarines were stationed in the south of France, patrolling the Mediterranean and the Adriatic, alert for signs of the Austro-Hungarian fleet. The Austrians had a few submarines of their own, and one of them, the *XII,* torpedoed the French battleship *Jean Bart* in December 1914, inflicting severe damage.

Germany did not like the way the war was going. Admiral Spee's squadron was mauled in the South Atlantic; four German capital ships were sunk, with the loss of more than 2,200 men. The armed merchantmen were a disappointment. The army was bogged down on the Western Front. The high command pressed for unrestricted submarine warfare, but the kaiser worried about its effect on neutrals, particularly Italy and the United States.

The high command got its way. On February 4, 1915, Germany declared that a war zone existed around the British Isles; merchantmen found in the zone, including those of neutral nations, would be sunk without warning. Germany contended this was the only possible response to the Allied blockade of Germany, itself in violation of the accepted rules of war.

Germany had only twenty-nine U-boats, most of them old, yet in less than three months they were able to sink thirty-nine ships. Each month their total increased, as did the revulsion of the world to the U-boat campaign. Then Germany made a serious blunder.

In the early afternoon of May 7, 1915, Captain Schweiger of the *U-20* sent a torpedo into the *Lusitania*. Twenty minutes later the British liner was at the bottom with 1,198 of her crew and passengers,

The sinking of the British liner *Lusitania* by a German U-boat helped draw the United States into World War I. Heavy submarine attacks on unarmed passenger and supply ships turned public opinion against Germany.

ML. LXIV NO. 20,923 · · · · ·   NEW YORK, SATURDAY, MAY 8, 1915—TWENTY-FOUR PAGES.   ONE CENT

USITANIA SUNK BY A SUBMARINE, PROBABLY 1,260 DEAD; TWICE TORPEDOED OFF IRISH COAST; SINKS IN 15 MINUTES; CAPT. TURNER SAVED, FROHMAN AND VANDERBILT MISSING; WASHINGTON BELIEVES THAT A GRAVE CRISIS IS AT HANI

:KS THE PRESIDENT

hington Deeply Stir-
:d by the Loss of
American Lives.

:ETINS AT WHITE HOUSE

n Reads Them Closely,
.t Is Silent on the
Nation's Course.

S OF CONGRESS CALL

of Lusitania Recalls Firm
one of Our First Warn-
ing to Germany.

'AL FULL OF RUMORS

s That Liner Was to be Sunk
are Heard Before Actual
News Came.

The Lost Cunard Steamship Lusitania
X Where the First Torpedo Struck.   XX Where the Second Torpedo Struck.

SOME DEAD TAKEN ASH'O

Several Hundred Surv
ors at Queenstown
and Kinsale.

STEWARD TELLS OF DISAST

One Torpedo Crashes Into
Doomed Liner's Bow, Anoth
Into the Engine Room.

SHIP LISTS OVER TO PC

Makes It Impossible to Lo
Many Boats. So Hundre
Must Have Gone Down.

ATTACKED IN BROAD [

Passengers at Luncheon—War
Had Been Given by Germans
fore the Ship Left New Yor

Only 650 Were Saved,
Few Cabin Passenge

QUEENSTOWN, Sat
day, May 8, 4:28 A M
Survivors of the Lusita
who have arrived here e
mate that only about 650
those aboard the stea
were saved, and say only
small proportion of the
rescued were saloon pass
gers.

Cunard Office Here Besieged for News;
Fate of 1,918 on Lusitania Long in Doubt

Nothing Heard from the Well-Known Passengers on
Board—Story of Disaster Long Unconfirmed
While Anxious Crowds Seek Details.

List of Saved Includes Capt. Turner;
Vanderbilt and Frohman Reported Lost

Saw the Submarine 100 Yards Off
and Watched Torpedo as It Struck Ship

Ernest Cowper, a Toronto Newspaper Man, Describes
Attack, Seen from Ship's Rail—Poison Gas
Used in Torpedoes, Say Other Passengers.

many of whom were children. Among the victims were 128 Americans.

The sinking touched off a fire storm of protest. Germany claimed the *Lusitania* was carrying 173 tons of ammunition, and advertisements placed by the German government in New York newspapers had warned Americans of the danger. This rationale fell on deaf ears. The *Lusitania* became synonymous with German infamy.

Shipping losses to U-boats fell off in the wake of the *Lusitania* sinking, prompting Churchill to speak of "the failure of the German submarine campaign." British warships sank seven U-boats, and experiments with acoustic mines and depth charges were promising. In March 1915 the *U-8* was caught in the nets at Dover and sunk. A few days later the battleship *Dreadnought* rammed and sank the *U-12,* commanded by Korvetten-Kapitan Weddigen who had sunk the three British cruisers, and Britain had something to cheer about. The cheers were premature. The worst was yet to come.

On August 19 another British liner, the *Arabic,* was sunk by the *U-24* off Ireland. Among the dead were three Americans. The U.S. sharply protested, and within days Germany banned attacks on liners, sending its U-boats to the Mediterranean and the North Sea. But German shipyards continued to work overtime building U-boats; sixty-one were completed by the end of 1915.

The number of U-boats in service wasn't the number in combat. Five U-boats were needed to maintain a combat position: one on the position, another on its way home, a third on its way out, one being made ready for sea, and a fifth in dry dock. In *The Great War at Sea: 1914–1918* author Richard Hough summarizes a German Navy report: "The large amount of technical apparatus aboard a U-boat required very careful overhauling and repair on her return from an expedition; also, the damage due to the voyage or from enemy attacks had to be repaired. Generally speaking, after four weeks at sea a boat would need to lie in the dockyard for the same length of time for repairs."

U-boats soon were back in the Atlantic, and shipping losses increased dramatically. In January 1915 U-boats sank 32,000 tons of British shipping and 15,390 tons of French and neutral shipping. By March the total had risen to 80,700 tons; by May, 185,000. Germany now had a base at Bruges in occupied Belgium, giving U-boats easy access to Atlantic shipping lanes.

Britain was feeling the pinch. In a way, so was America. The war economies of Britain and France had created profitable new markets for American munitions and increased orders for other products. But there was no profit if the ships carrying American merchandise were sunk.

The 1915 U-boat offensive prompted Britain to call up yachts, trawlers, and other craft, put guns aboard, and send them on submarine patrol. Destroyers escorted capital ships everywhere; there would be no more sitting ducks. But there simply was too much sea to patrol.

Smelling blood, the German Navy again urged unrestricted submarine warfare, claiming it would starve Britain out of the war in six months. The kaiser was tempted, but feared it would bring America into the war. A compromise was worked out. In the war zone enemy merchantmen were fair game; outside the zone they could be sunk without warning only if they were armed. Liners would be spared. The Navy reluctantly agreed, warning that U-boats would find these restrictions difficult.

The Navy was right. The renewed U-boat campaign began February 11, 1916, and less than a month later the *U(B)-29* torpedoed the French passenger steamer *Susan* in the English Channel. The *Susan* didn't sink, but many of her 380 passengers were killed or injured, including several Americans.

President Woodrow Wilson, through the State Department, told Germany that it must abandon "its present methods of submarine warfare against passenger and freight-carrying vessels" or face a break in diplomatic relations. The German response was to publicly call off the U-boat campaign, but the U-boats soon went back to their old tactics. The toll on Allied shipping again increased, exceeding a half-million tons a month by the end of the year.

The British introduced "Q-ships," decoy vessels with concealed guns. A Q-ship would loiter in a likely area to lure a U-boat to surface. When the Q-ship was accosted, most of the crew would abandon ship, leaving a secret gun crew behind. When the U-boat closed for an easy shot, the gun crew would open fire. The Q-ships sank a few U-boats at first, but never enough to justify their expense. The Allies also armed merchantmen; the U-boats responded by torpedoing merchantmen on sight.

Two effective antisubmarine devices came into service in 1916, the hydrophone and the depth charge. The hydrophone gave the Allies a way to detect the presence of submerged U-boats; the depth charge, three hundred pounds of explosives rigged to go off at a predetermined depth, proved capable of destroying them. In July 1916 the *Salmon*, equipped with hydrophones, became the first patrol to sink a U-boat with depth charges.

In 1916 a curiosity arrived in Baltimore, the cargo submarine *Deutschland*. Owned by the German Lloyd Lines, the 315-foot-long submarine had crossed the Atlantic in only sixteen days carrying 600 tons of cargo. Simon Lake, who had envisioned cargo-carrying submarines himself, went to Baltimore to welcome the *Deutschland*, only to find that it had infringed on many of his patents. He threatened to sue but was placated with promises of postwar contracts. The *Deutschland* returned home loaded with nickel, tin, and rubber, much to the annoyance of the British.

Germany felt that the visit was a propaganda victory, and a second cargo submarine, the *Bremen*, set out for Newport, Rhode Island, but was sunk by a mine off the Orkneys. The *Bremen*'s escort, the *U-53*,

During World War I, shipyard workers at Electric Boat framing a submarine hull pause to pose for the photographer. A number of Holland-type submarines were built, but few saw action in the war.

proceeded to lie off the American coast, sinking a merchantman within sight of the Nantucket lightship.

By early 1917 Germany was convinced that America soon would enter the war, and that its only hope was to force Britain to sue for peace. The German fleet had narrowly escaped destruction at the Battle of Jutland in May 1916 and was no longer a factor in the war. But new submarines were coming into service, and the average number at sea had risen from ten in mid-1914 to nearly forty. Unrestricted submarine warfare was resumed.

At first the gamble paid off. In April 1917, U-boats sank nearly one of every four ships entering the war zone, a total of 800,000 tons. In February and March of 1916, 1,149 ships had arrived in British ports; a year later, 300. Merchantmen were being sunk far faster than they could be replaced. Britain was down to a six-week supply of food.

Britain sought desperately for a way to stop the U-boats. It found one: the convoy, merchantmen sailing in groups protected by warships. Convoys had been used from the fourteenth century to the end of the Napoleonic Wars, but had been abandoned with the passing of the age of sail. History doesn't record who suggested resurrecting convoys in World War I, but it wasn't the British Navy. The Navy argued that convoys would require escort vessels better used elsewhere, that the logistics were too complicated, and that convoys would simply attract more U-boats.

At the insistence of the French, ships carrying coal from Britain to France were put in convoys, and sinkings dropped from 25 percent to less than one percent. Atlantic convoys worked well, too; losses to U-boats were cut in half.

Before the introduction of convoys, U-boats could lie in wait for a ship to come along; now they had to go to the convoy, fire off a torpedo, dive deep, and try to escape. Submarine captain Karl Dönitz wrote in his memoirs, "The oceans at once became bare and empty;

WHAT THE NAVY IS DOING

The 16 C boats On C... Many Miles on the Surface.

RECRUITING STATION
508 POST OFFICE BUILDING
CLEVELAND, OHIO

Seven Submarines Docking at the Same Time.

2, 3 AND 4 YEAR ENLISTMENT

Press of Navy Recruiting Bureau, New York

BE A SUB-MARINER

Work in submarines is interesting, technical and highly scientific. It is the beginning of a mechanical and electrical career, it involves the study of optics, of motors, batteries, electrical installation and oil engines. The Navy has many subs and just now a lot of keen eyed youngsters are wanted to become "monkey-wrench sailors". Promotion is rapid and for each dive there is extra pay.

THE NAVY ALSO GIVES EDUCATION, FOOD, LODGING, DOCTOR'S CARE, SPORTS AND AMUSEMENTS—BESIDES YOUR PAY.

A vintage Navy recruiting poster for the submarine service promises keen-eyed youngsters who want to be "monkey-wrench sailors" technical training, rapid promotion, and extra pay for each dive.

for long periods at a time the U-boats, operating individually, would see nothing at all." The heyday of the U-boat was over.

The early success of the German U-boats obscured the performance of the submarines of the other combatants. Until Russia left the war, her nineteen submarines were divided between the Baltic, Arctic, and Black seas. After Italy joined the Allies on May 24, 1915, her submarines operated in the Mediterranean. French submarines helped blockade the Dardanelles. Several Australian submarines supported the ill-fated landings at Gallipoli. American submarines made anti-submarine patrols in the Irish Sea and off the Azores, unglamorous but necessary duty. The number of submarines they sank was small compared to ship sinkings by U-boats, but still was substantial.

The terms of the armistice in 1918 stipulated that U-boats be surrendered in Allied ports. In a few months the vast U-boat fleet ceased to exist. During the war Germany had built some 360 submarines, and almost as many again were in construction at war's end. They sank more than eleven million tons of shipping and damaged nearly another eight million. The price was 178 U-boats sunk, 5,364 officers and crew dead—nearly 40 percent of those who served.

German submarines had come perilously close to turning the tide of the war, and the lesson wasn't lost on the major powers. They made submarine development a top priority in the years following the war. The Treaty of Versailles ruled that the Allies could use captured U-boats for research, and a number were distributed among the victors. The problem was that designers copied the wrong ideas. Germany had developed a large, clumsy cruiser-submarine that proved of little use in the war. Despite this, America, Japan, Britain, France, and Italy all developed versions of the cruiser-submarine.

Another idea that found favor was a submarine that could carry an airplane to scout for targets. In 1915 the *U-12* had launched a small floatplane off her foredeck. The American Navy in 1923 came up with a small seaplane that could be folded down to fit on a submarine. The British tried a variation, fitting a submarine with a catapult to shorten the time it took to launch a plane. Both countries abandoned their experiments, but the idea was taken up by the Japanese. They fitted a seaplane on their *Jun-Sun Type 1* cruiser-submarine but, like the Americans, found that it took forever to get it launched, then, like the British, installed a catapult.

Three submarines under construction as shipyards worked around the clock in World War I. American submarines saw little action, but sinkings by German U-boats nearly starved Britain out of the war.

The French also caught cruiser-submarine fever. The 361-foot *Surcouf,* launched in 1934, carried a seaplane and was armed with two eight-inch guns. The designers claimed a surface range of 10,000 miles at ten knots.

Some countries, notably Italy and Japan, experimented with midget submarines, capable of taking a torpedo into range, firing it, and getting away.

The United States and Britain decided independently that smaller submarines were more practical. Japan built submarines of every size. Smaller countries were building coastal submarines. By 1931 there were 245 postwar submarines in the navies of twenty countries, including Peru, Finland, Portugal, Rumania, Yugoslavia, and Chile.

At the 1921 Washington disarmament conference, the five major naval powers—Britain, the United States, France, Italy, and Japan—took up the problem of the submarine-building race. Britain tried to have the submarine banned. France opposed the measure, declaring that the submarine was the capital ship of the future. The United States and Japan also opposed banning submarines. The conference voted to permit Japan to increase the size of her navy, a disastrous concession in light of later events.

The London Protocol of 1934 set down rules for the conduct of submarine warfare that echoed those of the Hague Convention of 1899: the submarine must surface before attacking; crews and passengers had to be guaranteed safety, and could not be abandoned in small boats on the high sea; merchant ships were not to be armed, or use their radios to call for help or to warn other ships at sea about submarines.

Many publicly denounced the rules as unrealistic. Among the dissenters were Winston Churchill, who would see Britain again nearly strangled by German submarines, and Karl Dönitz, who would show the world that submarines make their own rules.

Between the wars the U.S. Navy was plagued with submarine disasters. On March 25, 1924, the first U.S. submarine fatality occurred when the *F-4* failed to resurface after a dive off Honolulu. All hands were lost, but a salvage record was set when the boat was recovered from 306 feet. The recovery also set new records for deep-sea divers. Two officers, George Stillson and George French, in 1907 had developed techniques that enabled divers to descend to 274 feet. Divers on the *F-4* were able to work at 306 feet.

In September 1927 a liner unintentionally rammed and sank the *S-51* off Block Island, Rhode Island. Only three men escaped. Another submarine disaster occurred in December 1927 off Provincetown, Massachusetts, when the *S-4* plunged to the bottom. Bad weather forced rescuers to stop their attempts to reach the survivors, although they could hear tapping from the six men still alive in the forward torpedo room.

The Navy moved to improve submarine rescue operations. Two important devices were developed: the "Momsen lung," a self-con-

The Boston Daily Globe

BOSTON, MONDAY MORNING, DECEMBER 19, 1927—TWENTY-FOUR PAGES · (2) TWO CENTS

More Help Wanted? Business For Sale? Advertise in tomorrow's, Wednesday's and Thursday's Globe.

Automobiles For Sale? Real Estate For Sale? Advertise in tomorrow's, Wednesday's and Thursday's Globe.

"PLEASE HURRY!" BEG SIX MEN ALIVE IN S-4 BUT WRECK CANNOT BE RAISED FOR 48 HOURS

Group Entombed in Torpedo Room Forward of Gaping Hole in Wreck Tap Out Signals With Hammer And Report Air Bad, But No Gas—Rescuers Unable to Reach Other Compartments But Hold Little Hope For Other 34 Men Entombed in Vessel

ARREST TWO MEN IN GIRL'S MURDER

One at Los Angeles, Other Seized in Nevada

Brutal Killing of Marian Parker, 12, Arouses Indignation

LINDBERGH SEES TWO BULL FIGHTS

Labor Parades, 100,000 Strong, for Him

Flyer Reviews Marchers From the Presidential Palace

MEXICO CITY, Dec 18 (A. P.)—

LOS ANGELES, Dec 18 (A. P.)—The police late today arrested a suspect in the Marian Parker murder case whose name they refused to divulge. Officers stated, however, that the prisoner is a young man of 26 years, the son of a Los Angeles doctor, a military school and university man, and known in the past to have committed offenses against young girls.

The police further divulged the fact that the imprisoned suspect was in a position to know intimate details of the Parker family life.

Acting on information which they said came from a confidential source

SCENE OF SINKING OF S-4, WITH BUOY MARKING LOCATION OF THE SUBMARINE

500 ROUTED AT LYNN BY FIRE AT THEATRE

General Alarm Blaze Does Damage Put at $50,000

Believed Work of Firebug Active in City for Two Weeks

LYNN, Dec 18—A general alarm

CIRCLES OVER SCENE OF S-4 DISASTER

Globe Photographer Flies to Provincetown to Secure Pictures Of Rescuers at Work

ACCIDENT DESCRIBED BY MEN OF PAULDING

Collision Lifted Destroyer Clear of Water at Bow

Submarine Periscope, First Seen, Was Thought to Be Fish Stick

PROVINCETOWN, Dec 18 (A. P.)—The submarine S-4 rolled over and a destroyer a craft, of-id today in miller, who lding at the the collision. but thought arker which a. I shifted w't want to umed in our of the sub. Then the

Salvage Ship Pumps Attempt To Fill Tanks of Wreck With Air, Lifting It

Pontoons and Derrick Vessel Arrive Today—One Diver Saved When Line Fouls

NO OTHERS BELIEVED ALIVE ABOARD CRAFT

Definite assurances that there are at least six men still alive in the sunken submarine S-4 came through to the Boston Navy Yard last evening when the divers communicated with the torpedo room by means of hammer knocks on the hull of the submarine.

The trapped sailors asked their rescuers to "Please hurry," and said that the air was bad. There was no evidence of life in any other room. On top off these demands came the news from Lieut Commander E E Ellsberg, who arrived at the scene at midnight, that it will take two days under the most favorable conditions to raise the submarine.

Rear Admiral Frank H. Brumby, commander of the control force, directly over the spot where the submarine is submerged, announced that "the air is now being hooked to compartment," following the report.

Tapped Code With Hammer

The diver used the regular Navy code with the hammer.

TAPS FROM INSIDE INSPIRE WORKERS

By JOSEPH S WARD Jr

PROVINCETOWN, Dec 18—Up forward in the torpedo room of the stricken submarine S-4, 100 feet below the tossing angry waves off Provincetown, are entombed a group of men whose number is estimated at from six to a dozen.

According to Admiral Brumby, the chances are one in 1000 of saving those who may yet be alive on the S-4.

"But my men will gladly offer everything they have to aid their trapped comrades," he said. "That is the spirit of the Navy."

In the after part of the ship perhaps more may be alive. This could not be learned today because aft of the conning tower a tangled mass of measuring wreckage proved an impassable barrier to the divers who risked their lives by the moment all afternoon, as they plodded their leaden way along the ocean's floor.

Control Room Bears Brunt

The two worst peacetime submarine disasters, the sinking of the *S-4*, top, and the *Squalus*, bottom, spurred the development of submarine rescue techniques.

Heartbreakingly, the bow of the *Squalus* shoots above the surface before sinking again, taking the six surviving crewmen to a watery death. The photograph is one of the most famous of its time.

tained breathing apparatus that would allow submariners to escape to the surface, and the McCann Rescue Chamber that could be lowered onto a stricken submarine. The chamber, adapted from a diving bell, would be locked into place over a special escape hatch built into the submarine's hull.

The chamber was put to good use after the new 310-foot SS-192, the *Squalus,* malfunctioned on a test dive off the New Hampshire coast on May 23, 1939, falling 243 feet to the ocean floor. Twenty-six men in the after section were killed, the other thirty-three were trapped forward. While the world watched, a rescue fleet was hastily assembled and rushed to the scene. Lieutenant Commander Charles Momsen, designer of the Momsen lung, was in charge of all diving operations, including the first use of the rescue chamber. All the thirty-three men were rescued in four descents of the chamber. The *Squalus* was raised and refurbished, and served effectively in World War II.

In 1931 the British explorer Sir Hubert Wilkins and the Norwegian oceanographer Harold Sverdrup attempted to cross under the

Air pumped into pontoons attached to the *Squalus* raised her from the bottom in an attempt to save the trapped crewmen. The disaster spurred the development of submarine rescue techniques.

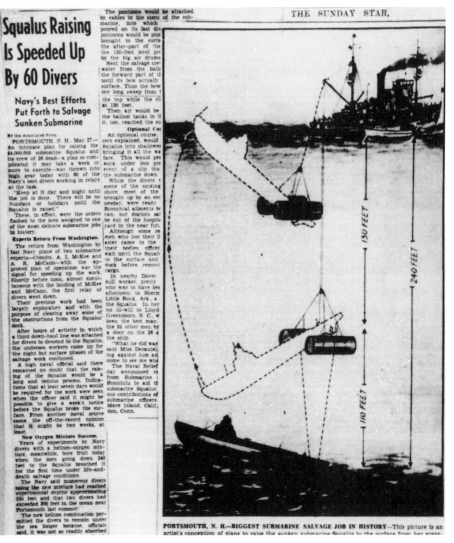

PORTSMOUTH, N. H.—BIGGEST SUBMARINE SALVAGE JOB IN HISTORY—This picture is an artist's conception of plans to raise the sunken submarine Squalus to the surface from her grave.

polar ice cap in a submarine. They obtained an obsolete fleet submarine from the U.S. Navy, renamed it the *Nautilus,* and with the help of designer Simon Lake added special equipment for the voyage—a pair of wooden runners mounted atop the superstructure. They planned to duck under the ice cap, increase positive buoyancy sufficiently to bring the runners in contact with the undersurface of the ice, then "ski" over it. There were enough gaps in the ice cap, they believed, to allow them to surface for air and to recharge the batteries.

There were flaws in their plan. Wilkins and Sverdrup tested the *Nautilus* under the ice and found that the runners scraping across the ice made a "quite terrifying" noise. Breakdowns brought the crew to the brink of mutiny. Two crewmen sabotaged the diving planes, but Wilkins and Sverdrup pressed on until ice formed on the hull five hundred miles from the North Pole. They gave up and went home.

Despite such ventures, submarines were considered first and foremost as instruments of war. In the mid-1920s the Soviet Union asked German designers to help rebuild Russia's submarine fleet. By 1939 Russia would have 276 submarines.

Between the wars, Britain built a number of 191-foot U-class unarmed training submarines. When Hitler's designs on Europe became apparent, they were armed with six torpedoes. When war came, the British Navy also had 19 fleet submarines in European waters, 15 in the Far East, and 15 Q-class boats assigned to training.

In the French Divisions des Sous-Marins were 28 boats based at Toulon, 17 at Bizerte, 12 at Casablanca, and a small squadron in the Pacific.

American submarine production was stepped up sharply when President Franklin D. Roosevelt signed the Naval Expansion Act. On the eve of World War II, the Navy had 103 submarines in service, 39 under construction, and another 43 in the planning stages.

The problem was that neither Britain, nor France, nor Russia, nor the United States knew the extent of the submarine construction program that had been going on for years in Nazi Germany.

Between the wars, many navies built experimental submarines that carried seaplanes. Like giant transport submarines and midget submarines, they proved to be either impractical or unworkable.

An Incident at Pola

In World War I the British began reporting shipping losses in terms of tonnage, a figure more precise than the number of ships sunk. Tonnage is a measure of cargo space on a merchant ship, or the number of long tons of seawater a warship displaces. The first merchant ship sunk in the war, the steamer *Glitra,* carried only 866 tons. By comparison, the light cruiser *Gloucester* displaced 4,800 tons; the armored cruiser *Duke of Edinburgh,* 14,000; and the battle cruiser *Queen Mary,* 27,000. At the height of the U-boat campaign, the Allies were losing more than a half-million tons a month, more than 500 ships sunk, averaging some 3,250 tons per ship.

Shipping Losses

During the closing months of World War I the Austrian fleet was holed up in the fortified Adriatic port of Pola, Yugoslavia, and the Italian Navy was determined to attack it. What followed was one of the more unusual incidents of the war, according to *The Great Sea War: 1914–1918* by Richard Hough.

Two young Italian naval officers trained in underwater demolition, Raffaele Rossetti and Raffaele Paolucci, built a 23-foot miniature submarine with external controls, which they could ride like a chariot. The boat could travel at two knots and carry 350 pounds of explosives in two detachable warheads. They proposed to ride their chariot into the harbor at Pola, blow up the largest ship there, and ride out again. The Italian Navy decided to let them try.

On a moonless October night, a torpedo boat launched the chariot a quarter-mile from the harbor entrance. Rossetti and Paolucci wore wet suits and underwater breathing apparatus. They slowly maneuvered through the nets and other obstacles and entered the harbor. The night was nearly over when they spotted the dreadnought *Viribus Unitis.* For some reason, a celebration seemed to be in progress aboard the ship. They attached the explosives to the hull, set them to go off in an hour, and turned to escape.

Before they had gone far, they were captured by a patrol craft and brought aboard the *Viribus Unitis.* They found that their captors were friendly Yugoslavians celebrating the collapse of the Austro-Hungarian Empire. The Italians told the Yugoslavian captain about the bombs. He ordered the ship abandoned. Rossetti and Paolucci jumped overboard and started to swim ashore.

They were overtaken and recaptured by a boatload of angry sailors who believed the Italians had lied about the bombs in order to escape. Rossetti and Paolucci were returned to the *Viribus Unitis.* They were being interrogated in a cabin when the bombs went off. In the confusion they got to the main deck, and there met the captain, who shook their hands and wished them luck. They jumped overboard again and from a safe distance saw the dreadnought sink bow first.

A hero's welcome awaited them in Italy. They were decorated for bravery and each given 650,000 lire.

CHAPTER 6

"He's the bravest man I know"

Karl Dönitz was born into a family of Prussian aristocrats, and the Dönitz men either went into the military or became evangelical pastors. In a way, Karl Dönitz did both, except that his gospel was submarine warfare. A highly decorated U-boat captain in World War I, Dönitz was one of the few officers retained in what was left of the German Navy after the war.

In 1922 German engineers started a submarine company in Holland. Spain, Finland, Turkey, and several South American countries placed orders, and the first submarines were delivered in 1930. German naval officers and technicians taught the customers how to operate their new submarines. The firm was profitable, but its real purpose was to keep intact German submarine skills and technology.

Soon after Hitler became chancellor on January 30, 1933, the Navy quietly set up the Antisubmarine School at Kiel. It seemed innocent, defensive not offensive in intent, but it was the beginning of the rebirth of the German submarine service. Students wore civilian clothes, and went to the Finnish island of Åbo in the summer to train on a Finnish submarine. At the same time, in violation of the Versailles Treaty, a closely guarded Kiel shipyard began building 250-ton submarines armed with three torpedo tubes and a deck gun. The school supplied the crews.

Hitler wrested military concessions from France and Britain in 1935, including permission to rebuild its navy to 35 percent of the size of the British Navy. Three days after the treaty was signed, Hitler authorized building 24,000 tons of submarines. In six weeks, the first submarine from the Kiel shipyard went on patrol. Five more submarines entered service at two-week intervals.

Dönitz was the captain of the cruiser *Emden,* although he had been instrumental in setting up the submarine construction program. He studied the role that submarines might play if Germany and Britain tangled again. Just as Germany was developing submarine technology, Britain, he reasoned, would develop antisubmarine technology. He assumed that Britain would use convoys again, and he had an idea that he thought would be effective against convoys. He called it *Rudeltaktik,* later known as the "wolf pack." Submarines would work as a team; when one submarine found a convoy it would track it, calling in the others for a coordinated attack.

When the *Emden* returned from an Indian Ocean cruise in the summer of 1935, Admiral Erich Raeder, commander of the German Navy, met the ship and summoned Dönitz to command the submarine fleet, which now consisted of nine boats.

Dönitz tested his wolf pack tactics successfully in the 1937 naval war games in the Baltic Sea, convincing the admirals that wolf packs would be effective, given sufficient submarines. He wanted at least three hundred submarines by the early 1940s, enabling one hundred of them to be on patrol at all times.

Under Dönitz the submarine service was transformed into an elite force. Every man was a volunteer, and the training was long and hard, physically and mentally. Dönitz resisted attempts to politicize his submariners. Their loyalty was to the Fatherland and to him, not to the Nazi Party. He would pay a price for this, for the Nazis held the military purse strings.

At the North Sea port of Wilhelmshaven, Dönitz established a headquarters for his submarines and outfitted it with high-speed radio equipment to stay in constant communication with submarines at sea. He devised a chart system dividing the seas into fifty-square-mile grids on which to plot the location of submarines on patrol. If he knew where the submarines were and could communicate with them, he could call every shot.

His request for three hundred submarines was pigeonholed. Hitler concentrated on rebuilding the army. Naval funds were spent on capital ships. Hitler finally told Dönitz he would have his fleet—by 1948.

Hitler invaded Poland, and Britain and France declared war on September 3, 1939. Dönitz then had fifty-six submarines, only twenty-two of which were available for North Sea service. He cautioned his captains to follow the London Protocol rules: warships were fair game, but merchantmen, and most particularly passenger ships, were not to be sunk unless they were engaged in military activity.

It didn't take long for the rules to be broken. On the first afternoon of the war the *U-30,* commanded by Lieutenant Fritz-Julius Lemp, spotted the British liner *Athenia* off the coast of Ireland and sent her to the bottom with a torpedo. Lemp had disobeyed orders by not checking with Dönitz before attacking, and nearly was court-martialed.

The British also violated the rules. First Lord of the Admiralty Winston Churchill advised merchantmen to immediately radio for assistance on sighting a German submarine.

Two days after the sinking of the *Athenia,* the *U-48* ordered the steamer *Royal Sceptre* to stop. Instead, the ship speeded up and radioed for help. The *U-48* sent it to the bottom. In response, the admiralty began to arm merchantmen. The scene was being set for unrestricted submarine warfare.

German submarines sank fifty-two ships in the first month of the war, including the aircraft carrier *Courageous.* They mined British ports, causing extensive damage to shipping. Destroyers sank the *U-39* when it attempted to close on the carrier *Ark Royal,* and sank another, the *U-27,* a few days later. But before the war was a month old, a German submarine shocked the Royal Navy.

Dönitz learned from one of his commanders that the guard ships weren't in place at Scapa Flow, the home base of the British Grand Fleet. Lieutenant Prien's *U-47* slipped undetected into Scapa Flow and torpedoed the *Royal Oak* as she lay at anchor. The battleship rolled over and sank, killing 823, including an admiral. In the confusion the *U-47* made it safely to the open sea.

In the aftermath of the sinking of the *Royal Oak,* Hitler personally presented Prien the Iron Cross, promoted Dönitz to rear admiral, and stepped up production of submarines. The chastened Royal Navy moved the fleet to the Atlantic side of Scotland until Scapa Flow's antisubmarine defenses were completed.

The first of Dönitz's wolf packs went into action in October 1939. It sank three ships the first day out, then found a convoy and, working in concert, sank three more. On the patrol, the wolf pack sank a total of eighteen ships.

Dönitz proposed building 56 500-ton submarines in 1940, 250 in 1941, and 348 in 1942. Hitler cut the plan drastically, not believing that wholesale sinking of Allied ships could bring victory.

In March 1940 Hitler invaded Norway and Denmark, ordering all available submarines to protect the invasion fleet. Torpedo problems limited their usefulness. Captains reported hitting British ships with torpedoes that didn't explode. Dönitz recalled the submarines from the Norwegian invasion to correct the torpedo problem, a decision that infuriated Hitler.

Crews waited in port while technicians sought to fix the torpedoes. After three months Dönitz sent a trusted captain, Viktor Ohrn, to sea in the *U-37* to test the corrected torpedoes. Ohrn sank 47,000 tons of shipping. The wolf packs were back in business.

In the spring of 1940 the Wehrmacht swept through Belgium and

Germany's Krupp shipyard managed to build U-boats almost to the end of the war despite intense Allied bombing. The snorkel breathing device gave the Nazis an advantage in the Battle of the Atlantic.

In the harbor at Kiel, the new war flag of Nazi Germany is raised on the submarine fleet. Hitler did not think submarines were important to the war, but their success soon earned his respect.

Holland and forced France out of the war. Now German submarines would no longer have to go through the North Sea and around Scotland to reach the Atlantic. Dönitz chose Lorient, southeast of Brest, as his new headquarters, with additional bases at Brest, La Pallice, Saint-Nazaire, and La Rochelle. Concrete, bomb-proof sub pens were built. Operating out of France extended the range of German submarines in the Atlantic 450 miles. In June they sank a record 260,000 tons of Allied shipping, nearly a ship a day. It was an amazing performance considering that only ten German submarines were at sea at a time.

A submarine accompanies a convoy steaming toward England during the early days of the war. Despite protective measures, U-boats inflicted heavy losses on convoys in the Battle of the Atlantic.

The failure of Göring's Luftwaffe to win the Battle of Britain was offset somewhat by the submarine campaign. Nazi propaganda sang the praises of the submarines. Captains were lionized, and their exploits thrilled Germany. Later in 1940 German submarines had two big kills in the Mediterranean—the carrier *Ark Royal* and the battleship *Barham*. Although Hitler didn't like Dönitz or his submarines, he finally was persuaded that they were crucial to victory.

A lethal variation of the wolf pack attack was devised by Otto Kretschmer, one of Dönitz's top captains. Instead of attacking frontally, he would submerge, slip under the escort vessels, surface within the convoy, torpedo everything in sight, submerge again, and escape. On October 18, 1940, Kretschmer first used this tactic, sinking four ships. Another convoy soon lost seventeen ships to a wolf pack that slipped inside and fired torpedoes from the surface.

Wolf packs bedeviled convoys throughout 1941, and the Allied losses were staggering. Churchill, now prime minister, declared that the most vital part of Britain's struggle was to defeat the wolf packs. The British were having some success. Prien went down with the *U-37*, and Kretschmer was captured when a destroyer sank the *U-99*. But Germany was building submarines at a record rate, and new captains were setting new records. A captain automatically was awarded the Iron Cross after sending 100,000 tons of shipping to the bottom, oak leaves for the Iron Cross on reaching 200,000 tons. Seven captains earned oak leaves that year.

German submariners were shocked in August 1941 when a new captain surrendered the *U-570* to the British intact. No German officer in the prisoner-of-war camp would speak to him, and several plots were hatched to kill him. The British renamed the captured submarine H.M.S. *Graph* and used it to penetrate German waters.

When Hitler invaded Russia in 1941, Dönitz moved his submarines to attack shipping in the Baltic, but the pickings were slim. Not until big convoys began the Murmansk run would the hunting get better.

A stroke of luck changed the tenor of the war at sea. In May 1941 the *U-110* was abandoned while under attack off Greenland. The crew set timed explosives aboard to scuttle the submarine, but they failed to explode. A boarding party from a British destroyer discovered an Enigma code machine with a list of naval ciphers for the next month. Cryptographers cracked the German naval Hydra cipher. Now Britain knew where the German submarines were patrolling.

America was entering the Battle of the North Atlantic. In September 1941 the destroyer U.S.S. *Greer* dropped depth charges on a German submarine and was nearly torpedoed in return. The U.S. destroyer *Reuben James* was sunk by a German submarine. Antiwar sentiment was running high in America, and Roosevelt did no more than express indignation.

Ambivalence about the war ended abruptly on the morning of December 7, 1941. Suddenly America was in a two-ocean war, ill prepared to fight either. Submarine defense was nearly nonexistent, and Churchill sent the chief of the Royal Navy's antisubmarine forces to Washington to give briefings. Construction was stepped up on destroyer escorts and escort carriers. But German submarines would make America pay for its unpreparedness.

Early in 1942 Germany broke the British and Allied merchant ship cipher. The Germans now knew the sailing dates, composition, and routes of convoys. Meanwhile, Dönitz shifted from the Hydra to a new Triton cipher, and the British couldn't crack it.

During 1942 U-boats sank more than six million tons of shipping. They cruised the eastern coast of the United States, sinking ships almost at will. Britain was close to being cut off from America. Dönitz believed that if monthly tonnage sunk increased from 650,000 to 800,000, the U.S. wouldn't be a factor in the European theater—whoever won the Battle of the Atlantic would win the war.

Late in 1942 British cryptographers broke the Triton cipher and soon realized that the Germans were reading the Allies' convoy cipher. Before this could be turned to advantage, a new version of the German Enigma cipher machine was put in service.

Escort vessels and a new long-range patrol bomber, the B-24 Liberator, were coming into service by mid-1942, but what changed the complexion of the Battle of the Atlantic was the Allied invasion of North Africa, called Operation Torch. Hitler ordered U-boats to the Mediterranean to harass Allied shipping there, reducing the effectiveness of the wolf packs in the Atlantic.

The fighting reached a new intensity in 1943. In March two wolf packs tried to trap convoy SC-121 in the North Atlantic. The battle lasted five days, and thirteen ships were sunk. The Germans cracked the new convoy code, and Dönitz sent forty submarines against two convoys steaming some 120 miles apart. The lead convoy of twenty-five ships was hit first; twelve ships were sunk in eight hours. In desperation the two convoys merged, but the submarines continued to attack, sinking a total of 140,000 tons before breaking off. The Allied escorts sank only one submarine.

Half a million tons were sunk in the first twenty days of March. From July 1942 through March 1943 wolf packs sank 784 Allied ships. The convoy system was nearly discarded.

In 1943 Captain Daniel Gallery of the U.S. Navy managed to capture the *U-505*. The secret code books in the submarine's safe helped

The German U-boat *U-505* yielded up important secrets after her capture by the carrier *Guadalcanal,* commanded by Captain Daniel Gallery. She flies the American flag as she is towed into port.

break the new version of Enigma. Now the Allies knew where the German submarines were. In April and May fifty-six submarines were sunk, another seventy-four in the following three months. Only fifty-eight Allied ships were sunk in that period, a dramatic decrease.

Other factors also played a part in the turnaround. Ships and planes employed in Operation Torch were returning to the Atlantic; advanced radar equipment made it easier to detect submarines; the newness of the wolf pack operation had worn off; and inadequately trained crews were manning the new German submarines.

Dönitz recalled his submarines in May for "regrouping." Morale needed to be restored and new tactics developed before recommitting the submarines to the Atlantic. Six weeks later Dönitz presented to Hitler the design for an electro-submarine, a streamlined boat with a "figure-8" hull and a large battery capacity to give it more underwater speed. A feature was automatic torpedo reloading—thirty minutes were required to reload manually—which would make the new submarine particularly deadly against convoys. Hitler ordered Albert Speer to have shipyards work around the clock building the electrosubmarine.

Another invention was the Walter turbine, which burned a mixture of hydrogen peroxide and fuel oil and would release sufficient oxygen to supply the submarine. The turbine could propel a submarine underwater at speeds in excess of twenty knots. Tests were encouraging, but the turbine never saw service, partly because of its excessive fuel consumption.

A device that saw service late in the war was the snorkel, a breathing tube that permitted a submarine to stay below the surface for indefinite periods. Late in the war, experimental submarines were equipped to fire the V-2 rocket bombs.

But neither inventive genius nor courage regained the German initiative in the Atlantic. At war's end, German submarines were being systematically sent to the bottom. As Russian troops entered Berlin, Hitler named Dönitz, now Commander in Chief of the German Navy, to succeed him as führer, then committed suicide.

On May 7, 1945, Dönitz radioed his captains to cease hostilities. Some refused to surrender and scuttled their boats. One sailed to South America to be interned, but most surrendered to the nearest warship to be escorted into port.

What had the German submarines accomplished? During the war they sank 175 warships and 2,828 merchantmen. Of the 1,162 submarines built, 784 were sunk. Some 32,000 of the 39,000 officers and men who served were killed.

At the outbreak of the war, Britain had 58 submarines, most of them of modern design. They fought a type of war quite different from the U-boats, working in shallow waters strewn with mines and close to enemy bases with concentrations of antisubmarine forces. They were after warships, but few ventured out of port and those that did were heavily escorted.

In the final days of the war, Karl Doenitz became Germany's Führer after Hitler committed suicide. Captured by Allied troops, he poses with his aides, Albert Speer, left, and General Gustav Jodl, right.

In the Mediterranean, British submarines operating out of Malta, Alexandria, and Gibraltar chopped away at Rommel's supply convoys, denying the Afrika Korps supplies during the battle of El Alamein. They also damaged the Italian fleet sufficiently to make it useless for the rest of the war. In 1943 British submarines went to the Far East and scored well against Japanese shipping.

During the war British submarines sank 6 cruisers, 16 destroyers, 35 submarines, and 112 other warships, and damaged 2 battleships, 10 cruisers, 2 destroyers, 6 submarines, and 35 other warships. They also sank 493 merchantmen and damaged another 109. The cost: 75 British submarines sunk, some 35 percent of the 215 that served during the war; 3,416 submariners were killed, and 360 were taken prisoner.

Paying tribute to the submarine command at a postwar memorial service, Winston Churchill said, "Of all branches of men in the forces, there is none which shows more devotion and faces grimmer perils than the submariner. . . . Great deeds are done in the air and on land, nevertheless nothing surpasses your exploits."

Submarines in the Pacific

Submarines played a major role in the Pacific from the very beginning of the war. In Japan's attack on Pearl Harbor, its submarine force provided reconnaissance for the carrier strike force. However, midget submarines failed to gain entrance to Pearl Harbor and four were sunk. Japan entered the war with some 75 submarines. During

Japan built an impressive submarine fleet, believing it essential to its plans for the conquest of the Pacific. Crews stand to quarters on five submarines tied up at a secret Japanese naval base.

the war Japanese submarines primarily operated in conjunction with battle fleets.

The attack on Pearl Harbor nearly destroyed the American battle fleet in the Pacific. Practically all the U.S. Navy had to fight with were 22 submarines operating out of Pearl Harbor and 29 stationed at Subic Bay, near Manila. These were immediately deployed to attack the Japanese fleet during the invasion of the Philippines, but their torpedoes let them down. Some were duds. Some ran so deep that even a zero depth setting sent them underneath their target. Others occasionally ran in a circle, striking the submarine that had fired them. The war would be half over before all the deficiencies were corrected. Only one Japanese ship was sunk during the Philippine invasion; the torpedo failure rate was nearly 100 percent.

Several submarine exploits in the Philippines captured the American imagination. The *Trout,* commanded by Lieutenant Commander F. W. Fenno, rescued several tons of gold belonging to the Bank of the Philippines from Corregidor before it could be captured by the Japanese. The *Spearfish* carried a boatload of nurses to safety, a feat dubbed Operation Petticoat.

Lieutenant Chester Smith became famous a few months later by taking his submarine into Tokyo Bay and sinking a heavily escorted 17,000-ton merchantman.

Intelligence gave the U.S. an advantage in the Pacific. In 1940 a team of cryptanalysts built a replica of the Japanese cipher machine, a breakthrough that led to the unraveling of Japanese naval and merchant marine ciphers. By the spring of 1942 the Navy could read parts of messages transmitted in the Japanese naval code. Combined with other intelligence, this gave a comprehensive and accurate picture of the battle plans for the attack on Midway.

Early in the morning of June 4, 1942, the submarine *Cuttlefish* sighted a Japanese tanker. Planes from Midway investigated and discovered the tanker was part of a huge convoy. Nine submarines fanned out, *Dolphin, Gato, Grayling, Grenadier, Grouper, Tambor, Trout, Nautilus,* and *Gudgeon.* Two other submarines—*Cachalot* and *Flying Fish*—approached the convoy from another direction.

The nine forward submarines attacked the Japanese fleet, and the Battle of Midway was under way. The *Nautilus* sank the carrier *Soryu,* and the other submarines accounted for two cruisers, four destroyers, six Japanese submarines, and more than a hundred supply ships. The Battle of Midway was an overwhelming victory for the U.S. Navy. Japan gambled heavily on taking Midway, but Admirals Chester Nimitz and Raymond Spruance, greatly outnumbered but armed with superb intelligence, broke the back of the Japanese invasion fleet.

In early 1943 cryptanalysts broke the cipher used to organize and direct convoys of Japanese merchantmen. Japan used a large merchant fleet to supply its troops scattered throughout the Pacific and to bring back essential goods: Japan imported 20 percent of its food, 24 percent of its coal, 88 percent of its iron ore, and 90 percent of its oil. Like Britain, Japan was an island nation dependent on imports, but unlike Britain, Japan did not realize how vulnerable her lifeline was to a concentrated submarine attack. The Japanese Navy neglected antisubmarine warfare, and didn't develop radar until late in the war.

Submarine launchings were almost a daily event as American shipyards went on a wartime footing. Defective torpedoes plagued U.S. submarines in the Pacific for many months after Pearl Harbor.

American submarines used wolf packs against Japanese shipping. Japanese convoys were small, so the wolf packs were usually three submarines. Commanders gave their submarines fanciful names— "Donk's Devils," "Ben's Busters," "Laughlin's Loopers," "Ed's Eradicators"—and they roamed the Pacific savaging Japanese merchantmen. Theodore Roscoe wrote in *Submarine Operations in World War II,* "The atomic bomb was the funeral pyre of an enemy who had been drowned."

Submarine captains, particularly Lieutenant Commander Dudley Morton of the *Wahoo,* developed aggressive tactics to minimize the effect of a malfunctioning torpedo; the "down-the-throat" shot, for example, which involved firing a full salvo of six torpedoes at an attacking destroyer at point-blank range. Submarines often attacked on the surface at night. They used radar to choose a position for attacking, and evaded the escort ships with ease.

A factor in submarine performance in the Pacific was the leadership of Admiral Chester Nimitz, commander of the Pacific Fleet. As a young officer Nimitz had served on SS-2, the *Plunger,* and in World War I had commanded the American submarine force in the Atlantic. He loved submarines and knew how to mount a submarine campaign. From a few sinkings a month, his submarines increased their total to sixty-nine, more than two ships a day.

On the eve of the Battle of Leyte Gulf in 1944, the *Darter* and the *Drum* bushwhacked a Japanese heavy cruiser squadron, sinking the *Atago* and the *Maya* and damaging the *Takeo.* In 1944 the *Albacore* torpedoed the new carrier *Taiho,* inflicting severe damage that led to

A four-man gun crew loads and fires a three-inch deck gun at a Japanese ship in the Pacific. Captains liked to attack on the surface whenever possible because it saved precious torpedoes.

her loss. Later the 62,000-ton battleship *Shinano* was torpedoed by the *Archerfish*.

Japanese submarines were much less effective. By going after warships, they exposed themselves to antisubmarine measures. One U.S. destroyer escort, the *England,* sank six Japanese submarines in twelve days. They got in some good punches, however. The carrier *Yorktown,* damaged during the Battle of Midway, was under tow protected by four destroyers when the *I-168* found her. The submarine fired a salvo of four torpedoes, sinking both the carrier and the destroyer *Hasmann.* In 1942 the *I-19* torpedoed and sank the carrier *Wasp* south of the Solomons. A torpedo damaged the battleship *North Carolina.* Near the end of the war, the heavy cruiser *Indianapolis* was steaming unescorted between Guam and Leyte when it was sunk by the *I-58.* Of her crew of 1,196, 316 survived.

As their merchantmen were sunk, the Japanese relied on junks and coastal vessels to move supplies. These small boats could operate in waters too shallow for U.S. submarines. But by 1943 there were three flotillas of smaller British and Dutch submarines in the Far East, and they pressed the attack within the ten-fathom line. They also sank the cruisers *Kuma* and *Ashigara.*

Japan used submarines to carry supplies to isolated garrisons. Special supply submarines, the I-361 class, had a surface range of 15,000 miles and could carry eighty-two tons of cargo. By 1945 most of Japan's fleet submarines were carrying supplies.

Japan built three 400-foot-long I-400 class submarines, the biggest in the world. They carried four floatplane bombers, and were meant to bomb the Panama Canal. None of them saw combat.

Fleet Admiral Chester W. Nimitz, a submarine officer early in his career, used submarines effectively as he drove across the Pacific in the greatest naval operation in history.

Seen through the periscope of a submarine, a torpedoed Japanese ship slides to a watery grave. Submarines devastated the Japanese merchant marine, speeding the end of the war in the Pacific.

In Pearl Harbor after a successful patrol, a submarine crew
poses with its homemade battle
flag. The silhouettes show the
number of Japanese warships
and merchantmen sent to the
bottom.

Growing a beard during long
patrols was common among
both Allied and German submariners. Beards were practical as
well as decorative, since fresh
water was always in short supply on submarines.

On the deck of the battleship *Missouri,* Mamoru Shigemitsu signs the surrender document ending World War II. From Pearl Harbor on, the U.S. submarine fleet played a critical role in the Pacific.

Japan had 2,337 merchantmen when the war began, 231 when it surrendered on August 14, 1945. Of the 190 submarines built for the Japanese Navy, 135 were sunk. Fifty-two American submarines were lost, about one of every four that served in the Pacific.

The nature of the American submarine campaign in the Pacific and the men who fought it can be found in the story of two submarines, the *Wahoo* and the *Tang.* According to Samuel Eliot Morison's epic, multivolume *History of United States Naval Operations in World War II,* the story began early in 1942 in Brisbane, Australia, where the *Wahoo* was being refitted. Her new captain was Dudley W. "Mush" Morton, and his executive officer was Richard Hetherington O'Kane.

Their first patrol was to Wewak, a harbor on the northeast coast of New Guinea that was being used as a Japanese staging area. The only map showing Wewak was in a school atlas. Morton enlarged a photograph of the map, traced the pertinent area on a nautical chart, and the *Wahoo* was under way.

Eight days later the *Wahoo* entered the harbor at Wewak and sighted a destroyer. Morton fired four torpedoes, but the destroyer evaded them all. Instead of crash-diving, Morton held his position as the destroyer closed at flank speed. When the range was 1,200 yards, Morton fired two torpedoes "down the throat" of the destroyer. The first missed, but the second hit dead center. The destroyer rose in the air and broke in two. The *Wahoo* made it out of the harbor through an artillery barrage.

Asked what it was like to look through a periscope and see a destroyer coming straight for him, Morton replied, "Don't ask me. I made O'Kane look. He's the bravest man I know." From the beginning Morton and O'Kane were a team; they thought alike and could

Richard H. O'Kane

exchange duties without missing a beat.

Three weeks after Wewak, the *Wahoo* found two Japanese freighters and sank them with three torpedoes. About to break off, Morton saw a troop ship, another freighter, and a tanker approaching. He sank the troop ship, crippled the freighter, then did an "end around" on the tanker, using the submarine's superior surface speed to slip ahead, submerge, and wait for it to come into range. The *Wahoo* crippled the tanker, but she continued to make headway. It was dark by now, but the hunt continued for the crippled ships. Morton caught up with the tanker and blew her apart with a brace of torpedoes.

Thirteen hours after first contact, he was getting the freighter in his sights when another destroyer steamed toward the scene. Morton did the unexpected, turning to head directly for the destroyer. The freighter headed for the destroyer, too, and when it closed Morton turned and sank it with his last two torpedoes. The submarine crash-dived and eluded the destroyer. When the *Wahoo* returned to Pearl Harbor, a broom was lashed to her periscope, the submariner's way of signaling a clean sweep.

The next patrol was to the Yellow Sea. In nineteen days the *Wahoo* sank nine ships, two sampans, and a trawler before running out of torpedoes. The broom went up again. The *Wahoo* was being overhauled when orders came through giving Dick O'Kane command of the newly commissioned *Tang*. When he left, it seemed in retrospect, he took the *Wahoo*'s luck with him.

Morton sailed the *Wahoo* to the Sea of Japan, the most dangerous area for an American submarine, and found it chock full of inviting targets, but every one of his torpedoes were faulty. He was seething when he reached Pearl Harbor. The admiral asked him what he wanted to do. "Load up with live fish this time and head back to the Sea of Japan," Morton replied.

His request was granted. But after a brief stop at Midway, the *Wahoo* made for the Sea of Japan, then simply disappeared. The Japanese said a submarine in the Sea of Japan sank four ships between September 29 and October 9, 1943, but the *Wahoo* was not listed among the American submarines the Japanese claimed to have sunk during the war.

Dick O'Kane and the *Tang* made the Japanese pay for the *Wahoo*. Using the techniques Morton and he had developed, O'Kane and his crew of eighty-eight sank seventeen ships on their first patrol, thirty ships before they were through. But it was the fifth and last patrol that earned O'Kane and the *Tang* a place in history.

The *Tang* left Pearl Harbor September 24, 1944, bound for the Taiwan Strait, a seventy-five-mile-wide strip of water between China and Formosa. Japanese ships went through the strait bound for the Philippines, where the Battle of Leyte was about to begin. Shortly after arriving, the *Tang* sank two freighters.

O'Kane sighted a convoy of three tankers and two escorted troop ships. The *Tang* sped ahead of the convoy, positioning itself so that the ships would pass broadside. O'Kane was in the conning tower directing the firing. The tankers passed first and were blown apart. In the light of the burning ships, the lead transport saw the submarine on the surface and swerved to ram her. With no time to dive, the *Tang* lunged forward at hard-right rudder, sliding past the transport with inches to spare as gunfire sprayed the bridge of the submarine.

Once clear, the *Tang* fired her four aft torpedoes. Meanwhile, the transport, concentrating on ramming the submarine, had plowed into the other transport. The four torpedoes struck the two ships, both rose in the air in a series of explosions, fell back, and sank. The *Tang* had sunk the five-ship convoy in five minutes.

The next night the *Tang* found another convoy: two transports and a tanker guarded by two destroyers. O'Kane moved ahead and waited. When they came into range, he fired two torpedoes at each transport, and all four were hits. As the ships burned, two more Japanese ships appeared. As O'Kane prepared to attack, the destroyers started firing. The *Tang* managed to get off three stern torpedoes before the second destroyer arrived and prepared to ram the submarine.

The first torpedo hit a transport, the second hit the other transport, and the third caught the destroyer, blowing it out of the water. O'Kane, with only two torpedoes left, decided to finish off a crippled transport. He fired twice to make sure, then watched in horror as the final torpedo swung around and headed back like a boomerang toward the *Tang*.

The torpedo struck aft on the port side, and the sub started to sink quickly by the stern. The conning tower went under, and O'Kane and the eight others on the bridge struggled to free themselves. As they swam away, they could see their next-to-last torpedo blow up the crippled tanker. The bow of the *Tang* jutted up out of the water for a moment, then disappeared.

The survivors started swimming toward the shore but were picked up by a destroyer. The *Tang* was on the bottom under 180 feet of water, thirty of her crew still alive in the unflooded forward compartments. An electrical fire broke out in the battery room, forcing the men to seal themselves into the forward torpedo compartment. Deadly gas from the burning batteries seeped into the compartment, which was beginning to fill with water. The men put on Momsen lungs and started out the escape hatch. Thirteen got out; the others were overcome by the gas. More perished in the water. The Japanese rounded up the survivors.

Nine more died in a Japanese prison camp. Only O'Kane and five others lived to be repatriated at the end of the war. On his return home, Commander O'Kane was awarded the Medal of Honor for gallantry and bravery beyond the call of duty.

Despite the anonymous nature of submarine warfare, despite heroic deeds lost to posterity because they were performed on submarines that never returned, the submarine fleet in the Pacific for its size produced more heroes than any other branch of the Navy.

John P. Cromwell

Samuel D. Dealey

Eugene B. Fluckey

The Medal of Honor

In the war in the Pacific, seven submarine captains, including *Commander Richard Hetherington O'Kane,* whose exploits are recounted in this chapter, performed deeds of valor that earned them the Medal of Honor, America's highest military decoration.

Captain John Philip Cromwell, commander of a submarine attack group, was patrolling off the Japanese stronghold of Truk when the *Sculpin* was severely damaged by depth charges. He ordered the submarine to surface. Captain Cromwell was in possession of information concerning submarine strategy and tactics, fleet movements, and Admiral Nimitz's campaign. Rather than risk capture and the possibility of revealing secrets under Japanese torture, Captain Cromwell remained aboard as the damaged submarine plunged to the bottom.

On a moonlit night, a Japanese destroyer spotted the *Harder* on the surface and closed to attack. *Commander Samuel David Dealey* watched the destroyer come within range, and sent it to the bottom with a torpedo. The submarine submerged, resurfaced, sank another destroyer, then slipped into the nearby Japanese Tawi Tawi naval base, where it sank two more patrolling destroyers. The *Harder* escaped to the open sea and the next day sighted an enemy fleet. Commander Dealey torpedoed the lead destroyer, then crash-dived. Five dangerous short-range torpedo attacks had netted him five destroyers.

The *Barb* sank a large ammunition ship and damaged other vessels during a patrol off China, then *Commander Eugene Bennett Fluckey* spotted more than thirty enemy ships in Mankwan Harbor. If he attacked, he would have to escape by an hour's run at flank speed through uncharted, mined waters. Slipping through the heavy enemy screen, he fired the forward torpedoes at a range of 3,000 yards. Bringing the stern tubes to bear, he fired four more torpedoes, scoring a total of eight direct hits on six of the main targets. An ammunition ship exploded, causing extensive damage to nearby vessels. Commander Fluckey managed to clear the area in the confusion. On the way home, he topped off an epic patrol by sinking a Japanese freighter.

Howard W. Gilmore

The fourth war patrol of the *Growler* was marked by frequent encounters with hostile planes and ships, but still *Commander Howard Walter Gilmore* managed to sink one freighter, damage another, and escape despite heavy depth-charge attacks. The *Growler* was on the surface one night when a gunboat came out of the darkness and closed to ram. Commander Gilmore ordered the bridge cleared. While waiting for his men to go below, he was struck by a burst of machine-gun fire. Several crewmen started back to aid him, but the dying captain gave his final order, "Take her down!" The *Growler* submerged, catching a glancing blow from the gunboat, but made it home safely.

Sighting a Japanese convoy just before dawn, *Commander Lawson Paterson Ramage* of the *Parche* penetrated the screen of escorting destroyers and launched a surface attack. A torpedo crippled a freighter; a series of bow and stern torpedoes sank the lead tanker and damaged the second. The glare of the burning ships exposed the *Parche* and it was fired on. Undaunted, Commander Ramage struck again, sinking a transport. Ordering his men below, he stayed on the bridge to direct the attack on the convoy. A fast transport closed to ram. Commander Ramage swung the stern of the *Parche* as the submarine crossed the bow of the onrushing ship, clearing it by less than fifty feet. Now in a deadly cross fire from the escorts with the transport dead ahead, Commander Ramage sent three "down-the-throat" bow shots to halt the transport, sank it with a final torpedo, and escaped unscathed.

Lawson P. Ramage

The *Tirante* was on her first war patrol when she entered the harbor of Quelpart Island, a Japanese anchorage off Korea. *Commander George Levick Street III,* sailing in dangerously shallow water, penetrated the mined waters despite the presence of patrol craft and planes. He sent two torpedoes into an ammunition ship, which exploded in a mountain of white flames. The *Tirante* was visible in the glare, but Commander Street continued to attack. His last two torpedoes sank two Japanese frigates. Clearing the harbor at flank speed, he slipped along the shoreline, diving deep to avoid a patrol boat. The patrol boat dropped depth charges, but the *Tirante* made good its escape.

George L. Street III

An Unexpected Submarine Trip for a Future President

As the war in the Pacific drew to a close, submarines were assigned an additional duty, patrolling combat areas to watch for airmen shot down by the Japanese. The U.S.S. *Finback* picked up a pilot named George Bush. He had joined the Navy right after prep school, and in 1943 became the youngest pilot to fly off a carrier. Bush was shot down near the Bonin Islands and narrowly escaped capture before being rescued. The *Finback* had just gone on patrol and Bush was aboard for nearly a month, during which the submarine survived several depth-charge attacks.

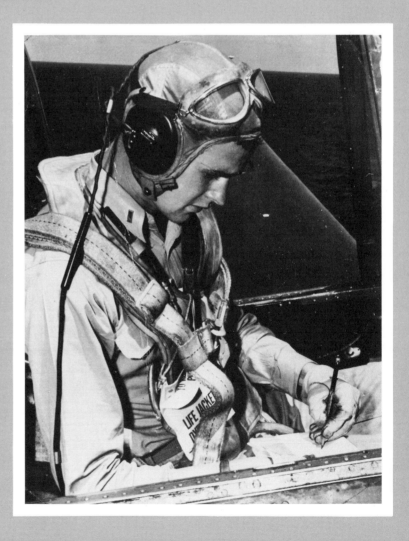

CHAPTER 7

"Underway on nuclear power"

In the early years of the Cold War, atomic energy and a human dynamo combined to produce the nuclear submarine, an event that would change the U.S. Navy as profoundly as the coming of steam. The human part of the equation was Hyman George Rickover, as unusual an officer as the Navy ever produced. He was short and slight, and looked frail. He commanded only one ship, a run-down mine-sweeper, and never saw combat. He rarely wore his uniform, and often publicly criticized Navy policy. The Navy had to be coerced by Congress into making him an admiral, and several times tried to force him to retire. He was fractious and unbending but a smooth politician. His mind could encompass the complexities of nuclear science and modern shipbuilding, and he had a vision: a nuclear navy.

Born the son of a tailor on August 24, 1898, at Makow, Poland, Rickover emigrated to America with his family and settled in Chicago. He was first in his class in high school, and shaved two years off his age to get into Annapolis.

As a young officer in the fleet, he was a loner, spending his free time tinkering in the engine room. After five years at sea, he returned to Annapolis and then went to Columbia University for advanced engineering training. He received a master's degree and a promotion to full lieutenant.

Rickover volunteered for submarine training and after graduation was assigned to the *S-48,* on which he spent three years. The next step would normally be command of a submarine, but there had been friction between Rickover and his superiors. He was sent instead to the Office of Inspector of Naval Materiel in Philadelphia and was put in charge of inspecting supplies and equipment. He continued his studies, writing an essay for the prestigious Naval Institute *Proceedings* on "International Law and the Submarine," which concluded:

"The submarine is the weapon par excellence of the weak naval power. Control of the seas can never be obtained through possession of a submarine fleet, no matter how large. But control of the seas can be effectively challenged and its exercise rendered hazardous by submarine operations."

Rickover became assistant engineering officer of the battleship *New Mexico,* helped his department win three Navy "E"s for efficiency, and earned a reputation as a fanatic. One officer recalled, "He had special plugs made and inserted in the shower heads, cutting the water down to a trickle. And then he started timing junior officers' showers. If he thought you were taking too long, he'd pull you out of the shower."

Admiral Hyman G. Rickover, the "father of the nuclear navy," was a fractious maverick, irritating Navy brass but getting results. No officer served on a nuclear submarine without Rickover's approval.

A pensive Admiral Rickover on the deck of a submarine heading out to sea. He fought against his retirement as fiercely as he did for a nuclear-powered navy. Typically, he is clad in civilian clothes.

Rickover then commanded a wooden minesweeper on river patrol in China for a few months. It was the only ship he would ever command.

A few years later Rickover was sent to the Bureau of Engineering, where he worked with officers as talented as himself. When war came he was made chief of the electrical section of the Bureau of Ships. He redesigned a number of parts and forced the manufacturers into making the changes.

In 1944 the huge Navy supply depot in Mechanicsburg, Pennsylvania, was mired in red tape and inefficiency. Rickover, now a captain, fired a number of supervisors and shaped up the survivors. Soon supplies moved to the fleet 25 percent faster. On Okinawa in 1945 he expanded the fleet repair facilities. His commanding officer said, "A more conscientious man never lived."

After the war, Rickover took charge of mothballing ships on the West Coast. He now could retire and use his executive talents in civilian life. But he wasn't through with the Navy yet.

In Oak Ridge, Tennessee, a joint military-civilian task force was finding practical uses for atomic energy. Rickover headed the Navy team. The Navy, one of the greatest users of power in the world, thought atomic energy could be used for ship propulsion. Rickover quickly grasped the technology of atomic power and foresaw how it could transform the Navy.

Control of atomic energy was being transferred from the military Manhattan Project to the new civilian Atomic Energy Commission. General Kenneth Nichols, head of the Manhattan Project, asked Rickover to prepare a Navy position paper. Hospitalized while awaiting a hernia operation, Rickover summoned his assistant, borrowed secretaries from the hospital, and wrote the paper in two days. It stated that the Navy could have a nuclear-powered submarine within the next five to eight years. The Navy said that was overly optimistic.

Rickover became a crusader, ignoring the chain of command to push his ideas to admirals, scientists, congressmen—anyone with influence who would listen. The Navy disbanded his team; he simply worked harder. The first breakthrough came with the Oak Ridge scientists, who started working in their spare time in support of his nuclear submarine. But he still had to convince the Navy.

He spent two months composing a letter to Admiral Chester Nimitz, chief of naval operations. He stressed the practical importance of a nuclear submarine, and how the Bureau of Ships and the AEC could work together to build it. Nimitz and the secretary of the Navy both approved Rickover's proposal, only to have it vetoed by the AEC. Rickover was given command of a new nuclear department at the Bureau of Ships.

In 1949 the AEC reversed its veto and created a Naval Reactors Branch under Captain Rickover. The prestige of the Navy was now on Rickover's shoulders.

Rickover pressured Westinghouse to develop a nuclear power plant small enough to fit into a submarine. By insisting that modifications to the prototype immediately be incorporated into a second plant, he cut months off the development time. The Electric Boat Company would build the first nuclear submarine, to be named the *Nautilus*.

Rickover now was a man possessed, as if he himself were powered by atomic energy. He drove everyone around him unmercifully. Nothing less than perfection was tolerated. Engineers could not get a single modification of specifications. Suppliers who did not come up with the exact items did them over or lost the contract.

Fifty-foot models of the *Nautilus* were built and blown up by miniature depth charges to test for weakness. On learning the Navy was using old submarines to test depth charges, Rickover had vital parts of the *Nautilus* put aboard. When they failed to stand up to the blasts, he blistered the suppliers for "selling him junk." The parts improved substantially. He saw himself at war, with "mediocrity, bureaucracy, and inefficiency."

Rickover was passed over for rear admiral in 1951. The next year the public became aware of the *Nautilus* project and Rickover. He was awarded the Legion of Merit "for meritorious conduct in the performance of outstanding services to the government ..." The next day he again was passed over for rear admiral. An officer passed over twice was expected to resign within six months.

A campaign was mounted to save Rickover. Senator Henry Jackson and Representative Sidney Yates spoke up for Rickover, and the media

Cutaway drawings of the *Nautilus* and the *Ethan Allen* show the evolution of submarine design. The hull has been streamlined for quieter operation and lengthened to house ballistic missiles.

Cut-away drawing of NAUTILUS (SSN-571), world's first nuclear-powered submarine.

ATTACK CENTER · BRIDGE · OFFICER'S WARDROOM · PERISCOPE ROOM · GALLEY · AFTER CREW'S QUARTERS · ENGINE ROOM · REACTOR · CAPTAIN'S STATEROOM · CREW'S QUARTERS · FORWARD TORPEDO ROOM · CONTROL ROOM · CREW'S MESS · BATTERIES · STORES

Cut-away drawing of USS ETHAN ALLEN (SSBN-608). Fleet Ballistic Missile Submarine. · Polaris A-2 missile, 1500 nautical mile range.

NAVIGATION ROOM · BRIDGE · CONTROL ROOM · MISSILE ROOM · MISSILE CONTROL CENTER · PERISCOPE ROOM · ENGINE ROOM · OFFICER'S WARDROOM · REACTOR ROOM · GYRO ROOM · STORES · BATTERIES · CREW'S QUARTERS · CREW'S MESS · FORWARD TORPEDO ROOM gave the controversy wide play. The pressure mounted, and in 1953 Rickover was made a rear admiral.

On January 21, 1954, within the eight years Rickover had promised, Mamie Eisenhower swung a bottle of champagne to launch the $65,000,000 *Nautilus*. The 320-foot *Nautilus* could travel underwater for more than 100,000 miles on the power of a nuclear mass the size of a baseball. The sea trials were a vindication for nuclear propulsion. The book *Rickover: Controversy and Genius* by Norman Polmar and Thomas B. Allen quotes an Electric Boat report:

"In many ways, *Nautilus* can be considered the first real submarine. Previously, submarines had really been surface vessels capable of submerging for short periods at best. *Nautilus* is the first ship whose natural habitat is the depths themselves."

Naval history was made in 1954 with the launching of the world's first nuclear-powered submarine, Rickover's *Nautilus.* The revolutionary vessel rewrote the book on submarine performance.

Admiral Rickover saw what a nuclear submarine would mean to the Navy. "The *Nautilus* is not merely an improved submarine, she is the most potent and deadly weapon afloat. She is, in fact, a new weapon. Her impact on naval tactics and strategy may well approach that of the airplane."

Except for its atomic reactor, the *Nautilus* was a larger version of the conventionally powered *Tang*-class submarine, with six torpedo tubes and a large passive sonar in the bow. And the *Nautilus* had a major problem: her cooling pumps could be heard ten miles away. A second atomic submarine, the *Seawolf*, was launched early in 1957, followed shortly by the *Skate*. Beginning with the *Nautilus*, atomic submarines would be called ships, not boats; they now had the size and power of surface ships.

The *Nautilus* set new standards for underwater performance. On one 265-hour underwater voyage, she averaged 19.1 knots, unbelievable by conventional submarine standards. Her finest hour came in the summer of 1958 in a top secret mission called Operation Sunshine. The *Nautilus* was ordered to sail from Honolulu to Portland, England, passing under the Arctic ice cap. At the same time, the captain of the *Skate*, Commander James F. Calvert, was ordered to sail to the Arctic to "develop techniques for surfacing in ice packs."

The *Nautilus* passed under the North Pole on August 3, 1958, surfacing beyond the ice cap five days later. Captain William Anderson radioed the historic message: "*Nautilus* ninety north." She was under the polar ice for 95 hours, traveling 1,830 miles. The voyage was perilous. The waters under the ice cap were uncharted, and the *Nautilus* was virtually blind, except for sonar and a television camera to look up at the ice. A hull puncture or damage to its propellers would have doomed the submarine and the crew.

The *Skate* passed under the North Pole nine days after the *Nautilus*. Near the pole she surfaced in a polynya, a sheet-ice skylight, using her great weight to break through the ice. The *Skate* broke through the ice eight more times on the voyage. In 1962 the *Skate* surfaced at the pole itself. Other polar voyages tested a new inertial navigation system.

New hydrodynamic theories were incorporated in the *Albacore*, an unconventional-looking submarine with a whale-shaped hull, a streamlined sail, and two propellers contrarotating on a single shaft. Inspired by aerodynamic research on blimps and dirigibles, the hull provided significantly higher maneuverability and speed.

The lessons of the *Albacore* were incorporated into the largest and most powerful submarine of her time, the $109-million U.S.S. *Triton*. At 447.5 feet the hull was longer than two average city blocks, and her nuclear reactors produced as much horsepower as the engines of a light cruiser. The *Triton* was launched August 19, 1958. As sea trials were ending, her captain, Edward Beach, was summoned to the Pentagon and asked, "Beach, you're about to start your shakedown cruise. Can *Triton* go around the world—submerged—instead?"

Showing the strain of command is Commander William Anderson, captain of the first nuclear-powered submarine *Nautilus*. Under the polar ice cap, he sent the historic message: "*Nautilus* ninety north."

On February 16, 1960, the *Triton* secretly sailed off on the route taken by Magellan in 1519. From Spain, she steamed south in the Atlantic, rounded Cape Horn into the Pacific, across Magellan Bay in the Philippines, then south through Lombok Strait in Indonesia, through the Indian Ocean, around the Cape of Good Hope, up to the coast of Spain, then across the Atlantic to the United States. The submarine surfaced off Delaware on May 10, 36,000 miles and eighty-three days and ten hours after her departure. The *Triton* surfaced briefly twice on the voyage, once to transfer a sick seaman, and off the coast of Spain to honor the country from which Magellan had sailed.

A helicopter took Captain Beach off the *Triton* and flew him to the south lawn of the White House. President Eisenhower presented Beach with the Legion of Merit, and awarded the *Triton* the Presidential Unit Citation. At the president's side during the ceremony was Admiral Rickover.

The voyage of the *Triton* had political considerations. It was timed to bolster American prestige at a summit meeting with Soviet leader Nikita Khrushchev. But just before the end of the record voyage, Russia shot down Francis Gary Powers's U-2 spy plane. Eisenhower refused to apologize for the U-2 incident, and Khrushchev walked out of the Paris summit.

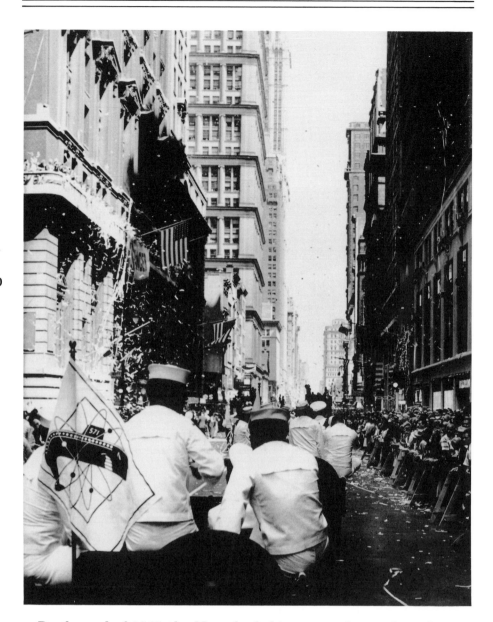

New York City welcomes the *Nautilus* crew with a tickertape parade. The first nuclear-powered submarine traveled 60,000 miles, more than twice the distance around the world, on a piece of uranium the size of a golf ball.

By the end of 1960 the Navy had thirteen nuclear submarines in service and another thirty-five under construction or authorized for construction. Three nuclear surface ships were being completed, and they would form an all-nuclear task force: the supercarrier *Enterprise* and the missile cruisers *Bainbridge* and *Long Beach*.

Admiral Rickover now supervised all the Navy's nuclear propulsion systems and, more importantly, virtually controlled all key personnel on nuclear vessels. He personally interviewed, selected, and supervised the training of submarine officers, many of the senior enlisted men, and the captains and engineering officers of the surface ships.

To be part of the Naval Reactors Branch required a personal interview with Rickover. The interviews were legendary, involving harassment, verbal abuse, and demeaning indignities. Critics said

Rickover's concern was with the reactor itself, not with the qualities that made great submarine commanders. Jimmy Carter recalled his interview with Rickover in his book *Why Not the Best?:*

> I had applied for the nuclear submarine program, and Admiral Rickover was interviewing me for the job. It was the first time I met Admiral Rickover and we sat in a large room by ourselves for more than two hours, and he let me choose any subjects I wished to discuss. Very carefully, I chose those about which I knew most at the time—current events, seamanship, music, literature, naval tactics, electronics, gunnery—and he began to ask me a series of questions of increasing difficulty. In each instance, he soon proved that I knew relatively little about the subject I had chosen.
>
> He always looked right into my eyes, and he never smiled. I was saturated with cold sweat.

In selecting candidates, Rickover often passed over Annapolis graduates for NROTC cadets who had majored in engineering, physics, or mathematics at leading schools. The program was designed to make engineers out of physicists, and physicists out of engineers. Rickover was leery of links to the "real" Navy. One candidate was rejected simply because his father was an admiral. There was no court of appeal; Rickover's decisions were final. Beyond talent and energy, Rickover sought total loyalty.

Rickover appeared so often before congressional committees that he was known as "the Admiral of the Hill." From the late 1940s to the early 1980s he positioned himself as the Navy's only true believer in nuclear power. A typical Rickover statement came in testimony before the House Armed Services Committee on April 18, 1967:

"We have got somehow to drag the Navy into the twentieth century. From the beginning the Navy has opposed nuclear power. Were it not for this committee, the Joint Committee on Atomic Energy, and the Senate Armed Services Committee, we would not have nuclear submarines."

No evidence supports the charge that the Navy opposed nuclear power. There is ample evidence, though, that the Navy opposed Rickover and his personal freedom. But Rickover apparently considered anyone who opposed him, what he did, or how he did it to be an opponent of a nuclear navy.

The Navy was eager to join the underwater capabilities of the nuclear submarine with the destructive power of the intercontinental ballistic missile (ICBM). In the 1950s the U.S. worried about the possibility of a preemptive Soviet missile strike against its land-based ICBMs. But missiles on submerged submarines would be immune from attack, ready to launch a second strike.

No place on earth is more than 1,700 miles from the sea, within reach of submarine-launched intermediate-range missiles (IRBMs). The trick was to keep a submarine on station months on end, fixing its position precisely enough for missile accuracy. With the technology of the time, to get a precise fix a submarine had to surface, which could betray its position.

President John F. Kennedy, a former naval officer, tries his hand at the periscope. The Cold War spurred the building of nuclear-powered submarines and arming them with ballistic missiles.

In 1956 work began on a system, named Polaris, to launch IRBMs from submarines. Scientists speculated it might take twenty years. In the wake of Sputnik, President Kennedy stepped up the program, and on July 20, 1960, the *George Washington* submerged off Cape Canaveral, Florida, and fired two A-1 Polaris missiles at a target 1,200 miles away. The report flashed back: "From out of the deep to target. Perfect."

Within the year the second Fleet Ballistic Missile Submarine (SSBN), the *Robert E. Lee,* stayed submerged sixty-six days to set a new record.

Polaris made the *Nautilus* obsolete. Unsuited for conversion to missiles, it was decommissioned in May 1980.

Two technical innovations made the Polaris system work. The SINS (Ship Inertial Navigation System) computed the submarine's course accurately, without reference to either magnetic or true north. SINS uses accelerometers and gyroscopes to plot all drift and movement in relation to a known point. Accuracy improves with additional fixes, but even one initial fix is adequate to provide coordinates for the missile fire control computer.

The second innovation was the development of an oxygen generator and "scrubbers" to filter and clean the air inside a submarine, allowing it to be re-breathed. With scrubbers a submarine could stay submerged on station for months at a time.

Polaris was the deadliest weapon system of its time. One submarine carrying sixteen missiles equipped with hydrogen warheads could deliver more explosive power than all the bombs dropped in World War II. The ballistic submarine is a doomsday machine.

In 1979 President Carter said, "As an ex-submariner, one who was in the initial program, I am personally biased. But I think that if there ever has been any one single weapon system that has insured our nation's integrity and security, it has been the nuclear submarines with a strategic weapon capacity."

The system has been constantly improved. The A-1 Polaris missile was replaced in 1966 by the A-3, increasing the effective range to 2,880 miles. In 1970 a new missile was introduced, the C-3 Poseidon with three MIRV (Multiple Independent Reentry Vehicle) warheads. Each warhead proceeds to its own target, creating a shotgun effect to confuse ABM (Anti-Ballistic Missile) defenses.

The nuclear submarine program has suffered setbacks. On April 10, 1963, the *Thresher,* the first of a new class of attack submarines, failed to surface from a deep dive 220 miles off Boston and was lost with her 129-man crew. In May 1968 the *Scorpion* and her crew of 99 were lost 400 miles southwest of the Azores.

Rickover once told a congressional committee, "If you want to have real responsibility you must make a competent man responsible for the entire project and not let him say, 'Well, I'm here two years and if something goes wrong it was the fault of my predecessor.' I can never say that. . . . If anything goes wrong, I'm responsible." However, on the night the *Thresher* went down, Rickover called the chief of the Bureau of Ships to make it clear that he, Rickover, was not responsible for the *Thresher.*

The rapid development of Polaris gave the United States a strong advantage over the Soviet Union, and the Red Navy moved to close the gap. The first Soviet missile-carrying submarines, the Juliett, and

The nuclear-powered U.S.S. *Thresher* was lost in 1963 with 129 men aboard in 8,400 feet of turbulent Atlantic waters 200 miles off Boston. The *Thresher* was the Navy's worst peacetime submarine disaster.

Echo classes, were no match for Polaris. But improvements came quickly after 1960. The diesel-powered Golf class carried the SS-N-5 Serb missile with a 650-mile range and could launch it underwater. The first Soviet nuclear-powered submarines were the 3,700-ton Hotel class, armed similarly to the Golfs. Between 1967 and 1971 the Soviets launched thirty-three Yankee-class submarines, comparable to the American SSBNs. Each carries sixteen SS-N-6 Sawfly missiles, with an estimated range of 1,300 miles.

The first Royal Navy nuclear submarine was the H.M.S. *Resolution* in 1967, and it was a curious hybrid: the hull were British; the missiles, tubes, and fire control technology, American. When the *Resolution* was commissioned, a wag posted a sign on the missile compartment that read, "You are now entering the American Zone."

France had planned to used Polaris technology, but poor relations with the de Gaulle government prompted the United States to veto the idea. An equivalent program was launched, the Mer-Sol-Ballistique-Strategique (MSBS) M-2. Five French nuclear submarines were built in the 1970s, and now comprise the Sousmarins Nucleaire Lance Engins (SNLE), operating in the Atlantic out of Brest.

Rickover, almost forced to retire in 1952, rose to the rank of full admiral and stayed on active service until 1982, fifty-nine years after his Annapolis graduation. No U.S. Navy officer ever served longer.

"Characteristics of Certain Submarines"

In his report, "The Characteristics of Certain Submarines," Commander Louis Roddis, an assistant to Admiral Rickover, presented these comparisons of the two *Nautilus* submarines to the Society of Naval Architects and Marine Engineers.

Date	1874	1954
Name	*Nautilus*	*Nautilus*
Length	232 feet	320 feet
Beam	26 feet	27½ feet
Surface displacement	1,417.6 tons	3,530 tons
Submerged displacement	1,507 tons	4,040 tons
Hull construction	double hull	double hull
Hull thickness	2½ inches	(not given)
Propulsive power	single; 20-foot diameter	twin screw
Propulsion plant	electric	geared steam turbine
Maximum speed	50 knots	"over 20 knots"
Cruising range	43,000 miles	62,562 on first core; 91,324 on second; 150,000 on third
Building yard	a desert island	Electric Boat Co.
Cost	£147,500	$65 million
Armament	ram	six torpedo tubes; some 20 torpedoes
Owner	Prince Dakarr of India	U.S. Government
Captain	Captain Nemo	Commander E. P. Wilkinson
Collapse depth	4,800 feet	over 600 feet

Sic Transit Rickover

Unwilling to accept forced retirement, Admiral Rickover carried his fight to stay on active duty right to President Ronald Reagan. In his book, *Command of the Seas,* John F. Lehman, Jr., Secretary of the Navy from 1981 to 1987, describes an Oval Office meeting he attended to make Rickover's retirement official.

President Reagan began by telling Rickover how much he personally admired his accomplishments and what a debt the country owed him. Rickover interrupted, saying, "Well, if all that is so, then why are you firing me?"

"Well, I'm certainly not firing you," Reagan said, "it's just that the Pentagon has recommended that it is time for a transition."

Rickover then launched a long tirade, recalls Lehman, resisting the president's attempts to calm him. After lashing out at Lehman and Defense Secretary Caspar Weinberger, Rickover turned his abuse on the president.

"Are you a man?" he shouted at Reagan. "Can't you make decisions yourself? What do you know about this problem? These people are lying to you. You won't get away with this. You won't get away without this hurting you. Don't you think that people aren't already using this against you? They say you are too old, and that you're not up to the job either. I have never seen anyone treated like I have been treated. No one has ever told me why I'm being fired; no one has ever told me that I am not doing the job."

Finally Rickover said, "Mr. President, you're too smart to be taken in by all this. You're a decent man, that's why you've been elected by the American people. Would you tell me right now why I've been fired?"

"Admiral, you're not being fired," Reagan said. "It is really my hope that you will be able to come to work to help the Administration . . ."

"Aw, cut the crap!" interrupted Rickover.

CHAPTER

8

"An infinitesimal atom floating in illimitable space"

The natural habitat of a submarine is the ocean depths, but until recently the ocean depths were almost as incomprehensible as the dark side of the moon. Man sailed around the world long before he knew how deep was the ocean, let alone what went on down there. Ferdinand Magellan, the Portuguese circumnavigator, attempted to measure the depth of the water at a point between the islands of Saint Paul and Tiburon in the South Pacific. His device failed to touch bottom, so he concluded that his ship was over the deepest part of the ocean.

A submarine theorist, Father Georges Fournier, wrote in 1647 that the greatest depth of the ocean "was about 400 fathoms," some 2,400 feet. Not till 1962 did a British survey determine that the ocean reached a depth of 37,782 feet in the Challenger Deep in the Mariana Trench, 200 miles southeast of Guam.

Ponce de León didn't find the Fountain of Youth, but in 1513 he reported the existence of the Gulf Stream, the giant river in the sea that originates in the Gulf of Mexico, passes through the Straits of Florida, then travels north along the coast of the United States before crossing the Atlantic.

Benjamin Franklin was an early student of the effects of the Gulf Stream. He noted, for example, that ships from the colonies reached England sooner than ships from England reached America. His interests included sea temperatures and sea life. Franklin is considered by some to be the father of oceanography.

In 1794 President George Washington appointed Captain Thomas Truxtun the first Oceanographer of the United States. Oceanography then was defined as the study of all the sciences having any relationship to the sea: geology, astronomy, physics, chemistry, marine biology, among others. Captain Truxton was one of the first to use water temperature as a means of determining location at sea.

In 1804 Nathaniel Bowditch, a mathematician, published *The New American Practical Navigator,* which still is a standard work. The first Navy hydrographic chart was produced in 1811 when the U.S.S. *Constitution* surveyed New London harbor. Charles Wilkes, a naval officer, was in charge of a scientific expedition that sailed around the world from 1838 to 1843 collecting data. He wrote books filled with information on deep soundings, subsurface currents, underwater temperatures, marine biology, tides, and the characteristics of waves.

In the 1840s Matthew Fontaine Maury, head of the Navy Depot of Charts and Instruments, devised a system of extracting oceanographic information from ships' logs to supplement the findings of scientific expeditions. As a result of his studies, sea captains were able to cut an average of 48 days off the 183-day voyage from New York around Cape Horn to San Francisco. Congress was sufficiently impressed with this to give Maury three ships for further oceanographic research.

In 1850 Maury's *The Physical Geography of the Sea* demolished the popularly held belief that the seabed was flat. "Could the waters of the Atlantic be drawn off," Maury wrote, "so as to expose to view this great sea gash, which separates continents, and extends from the Arctic to the Antarctic, it would present a scene most rugged, grand and imposing. The very ribs of the solid earth would be brought to life."

Maury pointed the way to modern echo sounders, or depth gauges, by suggesting that a bomb be exploded or a bell rung and the echo from the bottom be timed and recorded. A young associate of Maury, Midshipman John Mercer Brook, perfected a workable deep-sea sounding device to sample the bottom of the ocean.

Commodore Matthew Perry's expedition to Japan in the early 1850s produced a wealth of geographical surveying in Far East waters. Lieutenant Silas Bent made the first extensive study of the Kuroshio Current. Maury, while involved in surveying the seabed between Ireland and Newfoundland preparatory to laying the first transatlantic telegraph cable, it was learned that, contrary to scientific theory, marine life did exist below 300 fathoms.

From 1872 through the turn of the century, oceanographic expeditions were launched by many countries. The British ship *Challenger* made important findings. German ships explored the South Atlantic and Indian oceans. A Dutch expedition worked around the Indian archipelago; a Scandinavian expedition surveyed the Arctic Ocean and its approaches. The Germans and Belgians were active in the Antarctic. The U.S.S. *Enterprise* sailed around the world collecting samples of the seabed. And two useful publications were issued by the U.S. Navy Hydrographic Office: the first magnetic chart of the world in 1882, followed the next year by *Pilot Charts* containing valuable wind and current information.

The tide of oceanographic information was slowed by the Spanish-American War and World War I, but picked up again in the 1920s. Dr. Harvey C. Hayes, a scientist employed by the U.S. Navy, developed the sonic depth finder in 1921, and three years later the Hydrographic Office published its first bathymetric chart based on sonic soundings. The German ship *Meteor* made thirteen crossings of the South Atlantic from 1925 to 1927, taking some forty thousand soundings. The expedition yielded up valuable information on the circulation of seawater, wave movements and force, and sedimentary deposits.

Oceanographic institutions came into being in the 1920s: the University of Oslo's biological station, the Oceanographic Museum at Monaco, the Geophysical Institute at Bergen, and the Woods Hole Oceanographic Institution in Massachusetts.

The first oceanographer to capture the imagination of the public was Dr. William Beebe, a naturalist and the director of tropical research of the New York Zoological Society. He explored South America, Borneo, and the Himalayas before turning to the world beneath the sea.

Beebe was working on a design for a diving bell when he met Otis Barton, a young geologist-engineer with ideas of his own. They teamed up to build a diving bell, 4 feet 9 inches in diameter with 1½-inch-thick walls, weighing 5,000 pounds. The air supply was contained in the bell, two cylinders of oxygen and chemicals for removing carbon dioxide, but the bell relied on a tender for electricity. Beebe called the bell a "bathysphere," from the Greek for "deep sphere."

The inspiration for the bathysphere probably came from an Italian count, Piatti Del Pozzi, who in 1897 designed and built a spherical submersible named *La France*. The walls of his bell were three-inch iron to withstand the pressure at great depths. The bell, equipped with portholes and an electric floodlight, was lowered from a barge, and working arms enabled Count Del Pozzi to handle tools while working on sunken ships.

Beebe's bathysphere was built to go deep. In its first unmanned test off Bermuda in 1930, it was lowered to 1,500 feet. Then Beebe and Barton took her down. Beebe was fascinated by the blue world he saw outside the bell. "It excited our optic nerves in a most confusing manner," he said. "We kept thinking and calling it brilliant. . . . I brought all my logic to bear, I put out of mind the excitement of our position in watery space and tried to think sanely of comparative

Dr. William Beebe, left, and Otis Barton with the bathysphere in which they descended to a record 3,028 feet off Bermuda in 1934. The bathyspere looked like a giant iron globe with portholes.

color, and I failed utterly." They descended to eight hundred feet, well beyond the limit of visibility, before returning to the surface.

A floodlight was rigged outside the bell, and Beebe decided to take the bathysphere to its ultimate safe depth, 1,428 feet. Beebe used a spectroscope while descending to study the gradual disappearance of colors from the surrounding water. Red was the first to go at 20 feet, followed by orange at 150 feet; by 350 feet the yellow was almost gone; at 450 feet no blue remained, just violet and a hint of green; then at 800 feet only a pale gray. Outside the porthole the water was almost black.

Beebe turned on the searchlight to make notes on the marine life he found. At some levels there was nothing to see. At other levels the sea was alive with fish. The bell stopped at 1,400 feet, the water pressure now at slightly more than 650 pounds per square inch. Beebe said he looked down "into the black pit-mouth of hell itself." Quoting philosopher Herbert Spencer, he said he felt as if he were "an infinitesimal atom floating in illimitable space."

Beebe and Barton made improvements in the bathysphere and returned to Bermuda in 1932 for additional experiments, reaching a depth of 2,175 feet. They descended to 3,036 feet two years later, and continued diving at depths from 500 to 3,000 feet until the onset of World War II. No further records were set, but their purpose was not to set new diving records but to develop the technology of the bathysphere. They compiled a remarkable record of marine life at depths never before reached.

A Swiss physics professor followed Beebe's dives with interest. A month before Beebe's 2,200-foot dive, the professor, Auguste Piccard, ascended to a record of 55,557 feet in a balloon. Piccard noted that the bathysphere was dangerously vulnerable because it was lowered and raised by a single steel cable. He thought the bathysphere should be independent with its own buoyancy system.

By the late 1930s Piccard found the money to put his ideas into practice. The Belgian government financed his "bathyscaph," Greek for "deep boat," but construction was interrupted by the war. When completed, the bathyscaph was a sphere seven feet in diameter suspended below a 65-foot cylindrical float, which acted as the buoyancy chamber. The bathyscaph's hull was designed to withstand water pressure at a depth of 13,000 feet.

The French Navy's underwater research group sent observers to the bathyscaph's sea trials, including Jacques-Yves Cousteau. The thin-walled float, damaged in a preliminary dive, was judged too fragile, and the tests were called off. Piccard was in danger of losing his backing, but Cousteau worked out an agreement between Belgium and France to build a new bathyscaph with Piccard serving as a consultant.

Piccard had differences with the French and dropped out. He raised enough money for a new bathyscaph, the *Trieste,* and in August 1953 he and his son Jacques took it down 10,395 feet off Italy. Feeling vindicated, Piccard turned the project over to his son and returned to teaching. The *Trieste* had several improvements, including a forged hull allowing deeper dives, and a stronger, more streamlined buoyancy tank.

The French tested their bathyscaph off Dakar, Senegal, on February 15, 1954, taking it to a record 13,282 feet. The government authorized a larger, more sophisticated bathyscaph, to be called the *Archimede,* to dive in the unexplored Challenger Deep, where depths approached seven miles.

Jacques Piccard attracted the attention of Dr. Robert Dietz of the U.S. Office of Naval Research, who thought the *Trieste* might open up new areas of oceanographic research. The Navy bought the *Trieste* in 1957, beefed it up, and set out to beat the French to the bottom of the Challenger Deep. In January 1960 Jacques Piccard and Lieutenant Don Walsh, a submarine officer, took the *Trieste* down to 30,000 feet at a rate of three feet a second, then slowed to one foot a second to ensure a soft landing. They touched down at a depth of 35,800 feet,

Auguste Piccard, a Belgian physicist and record-setting balloonist, took his bathyscaph down to 10,395 feet off Italy. Scientists were astonished to learn there was marine life at this depth.

startled to see fish outside the porthole where the pressure exceeded seven tons per square inch. They surfaced safely, four minutes ahead of schedule. President Eisenhower presented Piccard the Navy's Distinguished Public Service Award and Walsh the Legion of Merit.

The *Trieste* was called into service when the nuclear submarine *Thresher* sank in 1963 off the coast of Massachusetts. It located the wreckage of the submarine scattered across the ocean floor 8,400 feet down. The submarine apparently had imploded.

The Navy built a bigger, better *Trieste II* in 1963, but Piccard returned to Switzerland to work with his father on a "mesocaph," a diving boat designed to work at middle depths. Failing to find sufficient financing, Jacques proposed that the mesocaph be built to take visitors to the international exhibition at Lausanne on an underwater cruise of Lake Geneva. The idea was accepted, the funding provided, and the *Auguste Piccard* became Switzerland's first and only submarine. It accommodated forty passengers, each seated in a swivel chair with a personal porthole. Floodlights illuminated the water outside, and closed-circuit television showed the passengers how the submarine looked from without. The vessel made 13,000 dives in more than 300 feet of water without mishap.

Piccard was retained to propose projects for Grumman Ocean Systems, and he gave them an ambitious one—exploration of the Gulf Stream. NASA joined in to study what effect virtual isolation for a long period would have on the crew. Another participant in the Gulf Stream project, the Naval Oceanographic Office, wanted to study the deep scattering layer, a strange phenomenon of great importance to submarine detection that occurs when sonic and ultrasonic waves are bounced from the surface to the ocean floor and back. At different depths, layers of unknown origin sometimes appear in the water and reflect the electronic waves, creating the effect of a false bottom, under which an enemy submarine could lie undetected. The layers rise at night and sink during the day, often as much as 4,000 feet. If the PX-15 could solve the mystery of this deep scattering layer, the Navy might be able to make improvements in antisubmarine warfare.

The PX-15 was completed early in 1968 at a cost of $2.5 million and named the *Ben Franklin*. It was a 130-ton mesocaph, 50 feet long, 10 feet across, and powered with four 25-horsepower motors, accommodating a crew of six. The vessel was equipped with a wide variety of scientific instruments. The captain was Don Kazimer, an ex-submariner and a Grumman underwater specialist, and Piccard was the expedition leader.

The Drift Mission got under way July 14, 1969, from West Palm Beach, Florida, accompanied by the support ship *Privateer*. The *Ben Franklin* dove to 1,500 feet, then floated with the current. Piccard worked the mesocaph at varying depths. Thirty-one days and 1,500 miles later, the Drift Mission ended at Halifax, Nova Scotia. The mission was a success in many ways, although the deep scattering layer remained a mystery. The accumulated data took years to evaluate.

Magnetic tapes provided sonic "maps" of the ocean floor. NASA received
65,000 photographs of the crew taken by automatic cameras inside
the mesocaph.

The Americans beat the French to the Challenger Deep, but a new
era of oceanography would star a Frenchman, Jacques-Yves Cousteau. He was born in St. André-de-Cubzac, France, in 1910, and it
wasn't long before his talents surfaced. When he was eleven, his father
brought home blueprints for a marine crane and Jacques built a four-
foot model from them. His proud father showed it to an engineer, who
noticed that the boy had added an improvement to the original design.

New understanding of the complex actions of the Gulf Stream
was produced by such craft as
the Grumman Aircraft Corpora-
tion's research submarine *Ben
Franklin* in the Navy's drift
experiments.

Cousteau graduated second in his class at the French naval academy and was accepted for pilot training, but was badly injured in an
automobile collision. Doctors wanted to amputate his arm, but Cousteau refused. For nearly a year he could move only one finger on the
injured arm. Returning to the Navy at Toulon, he slowly rebuilt his
body by swimming in the Mediterranean. In 1936 he took up a new
sport called "goggling," the predecessor of scuba diving. Cousteau
experimented with devices to extend a diver's time underwater.

After the fall of France, Cousteau reported on German naval activities for the Underground. For his service, Cousteau was awarded the
Croix de Guerre and the Legion d'Honneur.

During the war a French naval captain, Yves le Prieur, developed
a diving apparatus, a cylinder of compressed air carried on the back
of the diver with a hose to a face mask. There was no way, however,

Jacques Cousteau, inventor of SCUBA, ushered in a new age of underwater exploration with his *Souscoupe* (Diving Saucer), a self-propelled underwater craft capable of reaching great depths.

to coordinate the air pressure with the water pressure, which limited its use to shallow water. Cousteau went to Paris on forged papers to see Emile Gagnan, who had designed a valve to control the flow of cooking gas. They created the demand regulator, which released air to the diver only when he inhaled, and automatically adjusted to changing water pressure. This was the device that made scuba possible.

Cousteau helped form the French Undersea Research Unit after the war and raised money to buy an old British minesweeper, the *Calypso,* and fit her out as a floating laboratory. Cousteau and a group from the French Navy Group for Undersea Study and Research spent several years on the *Calypso* recovering Greek and Roman treasures. In 1953 this odyssey resulted in the internationally acclaimed book and documentary film *The Silent World.*

To free-dive beyond the depth limitation of scuba equipment, Cousteau designed and built a saucer-shaped underwater craft, the *DS-2,* nicknamed *La Soucoupe* (the Diving Saucer). The craft, its steel hull encased in a bright yellow fiberglass jacket, was powered and steered by two jet nozzles controlled by the pilot, who with a crewman lay prone on a foam-rubber pad, looking out through a small port. After testing well in shallow dives, the *DS-2* was put aboard the *Calypso* and taken to the Mediterranean. Off Corsica, Cousteau took the vessel down 1,000 feet—more than three times the effective depth of a scuba diver.

In 1962 Cousteau introduced his Continental Shelf Station No. 1 (Conshelf 1), a manned habitat on the ocean floor. Two scientists lived in its cabin for a week, coming out of the habitat with scuba gear to work underwater for hours at a time. Next came Conshelf 2 on Sha'ab Rummi (Roman Reef) in the Red Sea, the first underwater human colony.

Five marine researchers lived in the main structure for a month, working outside for as long as five hours a day in depths up to 100 feet. At an advance station, two divers lived in a mixture of helium and oxygen for a week, diving on compressed air to 363 feet. None of the divers required decompression during the experiment.

La Soucoupe was used as a taxi for the scientists. Compressed air kept out the sea from its dome-shaped hangar. *La Soucoupe* was hoisted to the ceiling and a floor put in place to permit mechanics to work on it unencumbered by scuba gear.

Cousteau and his son Philippe became television stars aboard the *Calypso.* A series of TV specials depicted their diving adventures on a six-year odyssey to the oceans of the world. Since the series began in the late 1960s, Cousteau has become both the symbol of and spokesman for man's fascination with the underwater world. "Man is just beginning to explore the seas," he says sadly, "and already he has discovered they are dying."

Since the end of World War II, the U.S. Navy has been an increasingly major factor in oceanography. In 1946 a Division of Oceanography was created at the Navy hydrographic office to collect and codify oceanographic information. The Office of Naval Research also was established that year, and it provides the main support in the United States for oceanographic research activities. A number of naval organizations now are involved in oceanography, providing a stream of information and technological advances that have benefited the submarine program in numerous ways.

Underwater technology received worldwide attention in the dramatic search for a hydrogen bomb lost in the ocean off the coast of Spain. A B-52 Stratofortress carrying four H-bombs was refueling in flight on January 16, 1966, when it collided with the tanker and exploded, the debris falling over a large area of land and sea. Lost were four H-bombs with the power of one million tons of TNT, sufficient to atomize southern Spain.

Three of the nuclear bombs were quickly recovered on land. To find the fourth, a massive hunt concentrated on twenty-five square miles of ocean off Palomares. Two deep submersibles were rushed to the scene, the 51-foot *Aluminaut,* capable of working down to 15,000 feet, and the *Alvin,* a 22-foot midget submarine owned by the Office of Naval Research, which could operate to 6,000 feet.

Other equipment used included the two-man submersible Cubmarine, five "acoustic fish," the Ocean Bottom Scanning Sonar, a Decca

Alvin is lowered into the Atlantic to search for a lost hydrogen bomb. The two-man research submarine located the bomb five miles off the coast of Palomares, Spain, on April 7, 1966.

SPAIN

PALOMARES BEACH

Garrucha

5 Miles

Mediterranean Sea

2,500 Feet

'H' BOMB

J. CARLTON

Directed by underwater television, a CURV (Controlled Unmanned Recovery Vehicle) was able to attach a cable to the hydrogen bomb nearly buried on the ocean floor off the coast of Spain.

radio navigation system for charting the search from shore, and underwater television cameras towed on diving sleds. A formidable task lay ahead. Admiral William S. Guest, in charge of the operation, told the press, "It isn't like looking for a needle in a haystack. It's like looking for the eye of a needle in a field of haystacks in the dark."

After nearly two months of round-the-clock dives, the *Alvin* spotted the missing H-bomb at 2,650 feet, still attached to its 60-foot-long

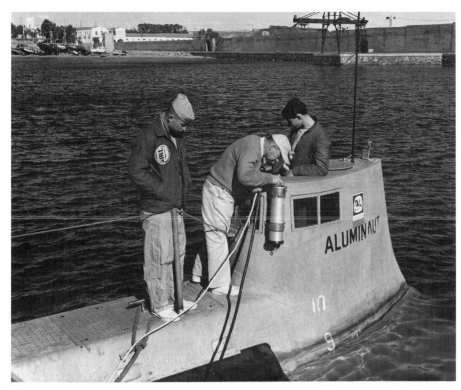

The *Aluminaut* also participated
in the search for the lost hydrogen bomb. The versatile 51-foot
aluminum research submarine
can lift more than 5,000 pounds
from a depth of 2,800 feet.

A crane lowers the Navy's
cable-controlled Underwater
Recovery Vehicle. Tanklike
treads enable the vehicle to
crawl along the ocean floor.
Recovering practice torpedoes is
among its many tasks.

parachute canopy. Both bomb and canopy were almost completely
buried in loose silt. In an attempt to hoist the bomb to the surface, it
slipped loose, fell to the bottom, and was lost again. The *Alvin* took
several days to relocate the bomb at 2,800 feet on the edge of a slope.

The CURV (Cable-controlled Underwater Research Vessel), its claws
monitored by on-board television cameras and operated remotely from
the surface, was called into service, but by the time it was in position

the bomb was gone. The *Alvin* relocated the bomb 300 yards away. The CURV was maneuvered into position to attach cables to the bomb.

Suddenly an ocean current billowed the parachute canopy, enshrouding the CURV's engines so tightly that it couldn't move. Admiral Guest ordered the cables winched tight to see if the CURV could be pulled free. The cables grew taut, then slackened. The winch slowly reeled in the cables. The *Alvin* radioed that it saw the CURV, with the parachute and bomb still attached, 400 feet off the bottom. The winch started up again, bringing the cables in a few feet a second. At last the CURV broke the surface, then the parachute appeared, and finally the H-bomb. It was swung aboard a Navy ship, two months and twenty-one days after it was lost.

During the underwater search for the missing H-bomb, the public became familiar with Deep Research Vessels (D/RVs) through the work of the *Aluminaut* and the *Alvin*. There are now some one hundred D/RVs in the world, half of them in the United States. Most were built by aerospace companies, and they look it. With their brightly colored acrylic domes and large external mechanical arms, they would seem as much at home on Mars as on the ocean floor. They are submersibles, not submarines, and require surface support vessels. D/RVs are used to make observations and gather samples, often at great depths. Although they share a basic purpose, no two D/RVs are alike.

Other D/RVs include a number of Perry Submersibles, the Cubmarines, designed for observation and salvage work at mid-depth ranges on the continental shelf. The Shell Oil Company uses its Shelf Diver to inspect underwater pipe lines. The vessel has twenty-five viewports, two drills for core and rock, a mechanical arm, and television cameras.

A D/RV that has been used extensively by the Navy is *Deep Star 4000,* designed by Cousteau and built under his guidance by Westinghouse. The 18-foot, 9-ton vessel can operate at depths down to 4,000 feet. Westinghouse built a successor, the 36-foot, 32-ton *Deep Star 20,000* for searches down to 20,000 feet.

Cousteau built *Diving Saucer SP-3000* in 1970 for his own use, a 20-foot, 12-ton D/RV capable of operating at 9,000-foot depths. An unusual D/RV was designed and built by the Navy, the 66-inch acrylic sphere *Nemo* that sits atop disks containing its life-support system. *Nemo* operates on a cable anchored to the ocean floor, and two crewmen can winch the bell up or down. The Navy also designed and built *Deep View,* the first D/RV with its entire bow section capped with a glass hemisphere. The 16½-foot, nearly 6-ton vessel is propelled by four electric motors and can dive to 1,500 feet.

The Navy's first Deep Sea Rescue Vehicle, the DSRV-1, was launched in 1970 to search out a downed nuclear submarine, link itself to the submarine's escape hatch, and take the crew to the surface, twenty-four at a time. The vessel is 50 feet long with a torpedo-shaped fiberglass hull, and can operate 3,500 feet down. In 1971 Lockheed built the DSRV-2, operational to 5,000 feet. Both DSRVs can be transported by air, and can be carried on a nuclear submarine, which can launch and recover them without surfacing. Both soon were called to the rescue in an underwater tragedy.

The *Johnson-Sea-Link* was a 23-foot, 9-ton DRV designed by Edwin Link and financed by industrialist J. Seward Johnson. On June 17,

Deepstar 4000's array of specialized instruments enables scientists to study and record phenomena of the ocean floor at depths up to 4,000 feet in the Navy's oceanographic research program.

Deepstar 4000 is leased by the Navy from Westinghouse to conduct oceanographic research. Knowledge of the ocean depths and currents is vital to successful submarine warfare in the nuclear age.

A deep submergence rescue vehicle rides piggyback on the U.S.S. *Pintado* in a "mother submarine" training operation. The submarine directs the underwater operation of the submersible.

A deep sea research vehicle can dive to 3,500 feet, couple with a stricken submarine, and take aboard as many as 24 crewmen. A DSRV is carried, launched, and recovered from a mother submarine.

1973, Link's son, Clayton, and three other men were in the DRV off Key West working at a depth of 360 feet near a sunken destroyer. Suddenly a strong current swept the *Sea-Link* off course and entangled it among the wreck's cables and debris. The pilot, Archibald Menzies, couldn't get the DRV free and radioed for help.

Five hours later the Navy submarine rescue vessel *Tringa* was in position, but the crew of the *Sea-Link* was having trouble with the air supply. The *Sea-Link* had two compartments, two men in each, with no access from one compartment to another. The "scrubbers" that purified the air weren't working properly, and Link and Menzies in their separate compartments made emergency repairs.

Deep-sea divers made three futile attempts to reach the stricken vessel, once coming within ten feet before being driven back by the current and debris. The submarine *Amberjack* arrived the next morning with two small submersibles. They were launched, but one malfunctioned and the other was unable to reach the *Sea-Link*. A

116

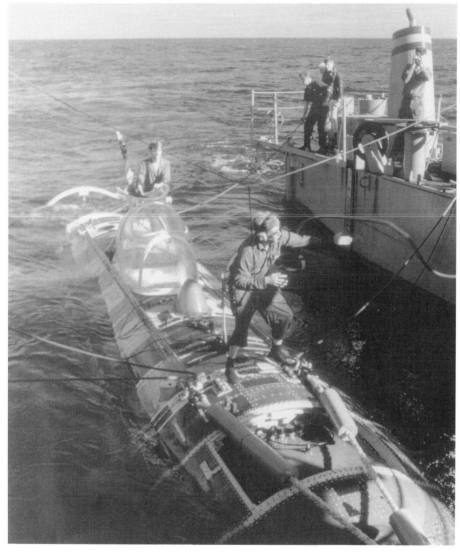

Somewhere in the Pacific, a
deep submergence rescue vehicle returns to the well of the
research vessel *Transquest*.
Survival on a stricken submarine may well depend on such
submersibles.

Navy diving bell was flown in, and two scuba divers took her down
but couldn't reach the DRV either.

The oceanographic research ship *A. B. Wood* arrived and lowered
a closed-circuit television camera. Menzies saw it and talked it into
position over the radio. The camera was hauled up, a grapple hook
was attached to the camera cable, and relowered. Again Menzies talked
it into position, and a few minutes later the *Sea-Link* was hauled to
the surface. Menzies and one other survived; Link and another crewman were dead from carbon-dioxide poisoning.

In another incident, a Navy unmanned CURV was flown to the
rescue in October 1973 when the 29-foot submersible *Pisces* sank in
1,375 feet of water off the coast of Ireland. The CURV, similar to the
one that pulled up the lost H-bomb, dived and was directed from the
surface by its closed-circuit television camera. It attached a cable to
the *Pisces* and it was hoisted to the surface. The two crewmen were
saved, despite a nearly seventy-six-hour ordeal.

An important scientific study was launched in 1974: Project FAMOUS, an acronym for the French-American Mid-Ocean Undersea Study. The subject: the largest physical feature of the earth, a 40,000-mile ridge that girdles the globe and bisects the Atlantic Ocean. In the valley that runs along the ridge, scientists believe, volcanic activity forms new seabed. Perhaps the findings of Project FAMOUS would link this volcanic activity to the phenomenon of continental drift. Geologists aren't sure whether in continental drift the earth's plates are pushed apart by the surge of lava or pulled apart by other forces. If the plates were pushed, Project FAMOUS would find telltale signs, buckled crust and piles of lava.

The site of Project FAMOUS was a section of the range and rift valley 250 miles south of the Azores. The American team used the *Alvin,* recently refitted with a titanium hull that extended her operational range to 12,000 feet. The French used the bathyscaph

How the Oceans Affect Submarine Performance

The waters of the oceans are constantly in motion, creating phenomena similar to weather in the atmosphere. It is more difficult to predict ocean phenomena than the weather, because only a few ocean conditions are visible, such as surface waves, ice, and tides. Predicting ocean phenomena, however, is necessary for submarines to operate effectively.

The waters of the oceans change from area to area and depth to depth in varying ways. There are changes in salinity, temperature, subsurface currents and countercurrents, and the existence of macro- and microorganisms. All these affect the acoustical and optical properties of the water, as do the noises of other ships, harbor activity, off-shore oil drilling, and pollution.

The ocean depths are impervious to light, but not to sound. Sound can travel a great distance through water at a speed that varies with pressure, temperature, and salinity. The average speed of sound in water is 4,757 feet per second, roughly four times the speed of sound in the air. Sonar is based on the principle that underwater sound transmissions are reflected by any solid object, and a sensitive receiver can detect these echoes. But the detection of an echo is just the beginning. Determining where the reflecting object is, and what it is, demands precise instruments and skillful interpretation.

The temperature of the ocean drops with the depth, but it doesn't drop evenly. The sun heats the surface layer, the depth of which varies by location from more than three hundred feet in the high latitudes to less than a third of that near the equator.

L'Archimede and the *Cyana*, once Cousteau's *Diving Saucer SP 3000*.

After repeated dives to the seabed 9,000 feet below, the scientists found a variety of lava formations in a 500-foot section of the valley indicating recent volcanic eruptions, but nothing suggesting seabed movement. Instead, there were many fissures and rips indicating that the bottom had been literally wrenched apart. An unusually large amount of sea life was observed, and samples from the bottom were rich in iron and manganese. This suggested to the scientists that there might be thermal springs in the rift valley, but a search didn't locate them.

During the summer-long exploration, the three submersibles collected a mass of samples and data. The *Alvin* alone brought back 867 pounds of rocks and took some 17,000 of the 50,000 exhibition photographs. Project FAMOUS was a major step forward in man's understanding of the underwater environment.

Below the surface layer are other layers, some as thin as two inches. The temperature will be constant within a layer, then drop sharply in the next lower layer. Finally there is the permanent thermocline where temperatures drop at a more gradual and even rate to the bottom.

The depth at which the thermocline begins also varies in different latitudes. It is found at 984 to 1,312 feet near the equator, at 1,640 to 3,280 feet in subtropical areas. There is a seasonal thermocline above the permanent thermocline, and in some areas there is a diurnal thermocline called the afternoon effect because of the time of day it occurs.

The density of the water varies from layer to layer. Certain organic and inorganic materials collect in the layers because they can descend no farther. The organic material is mostly planktonic, which attracts great numbers of fish and shrimp. The inorganic material includes erosion from the land and the ocean bed and debris. Organic and inorganic materials in the water can be difficult to detect.

Another variant is salinity. Melting ice, ice-floe formation and evaporation, rainfall, and rivers can cause salinity to vary between thirty-two and thirty-seven parts per thousand. This has an operational significance for submarines because they ride deeper and submerge easier the lower the salinity content. Captains have to compensate for the salinity content when operating near river estuaries or fjords, for example, or in seas such as the Baltic that are more saline than the ocean.

When both temperature and salinity change abruptly, the combination can produce severe underwater turbulence. Such turbulence may have caused the loss of the *Thresher* in 1963. Operating 220 miles east of Cape Cod, the submarine suddenly was driven down to a depth where its hull imploded. These areas of underwater turbulence also adversely affect a submarine's sonar performance.

The salinity of the water affects a submarine in another way: the increase in pressure with depth. In seawater, pressure increases by 44.45 pounds per square inch for every one hundred feet in depth; in fresh water, 43.50 pounds per square inch. The amount of pressure the hull can withstand determines the depth to which a submarine can operate.

A submarine can escape detection at the bottom of the ocean if the terrain is rocky and irregular. These irregularities will confuse antisubmarine sonar with an effect known as reverberation. A captain familiar with the terrain of the seabed knows where he can hide. He also needs to know the location of the continental shelf in order to rise over it when returning from a deep ocean patrol.

Surface conditions are a problem for sonobuoys. To the degree they drift from the impact point, they lose accuracy in fixes on a target. Under certain conditions, a sonobuoy moving with the current will report a stationary target as moving in the opposite direction. Sonobuoys also are affected by waves. Ten-foot waves produce a 75 percent loss in transmission; fifteen-foot waves make transmission impossible. Waves also affect the thermocline by mixing waters above and below the dividing line. This increases the noise picked up by a submarine's sonar system. Thunder and rain on the surface also increase sonar noise.

Sound waves in the ocean travel in arcs, not in straight lines, a phenomenon known as Snell's Law. When a sound wave travels from one density layer to another, its path is bent toward the normal when it enters a layer of greater density, away from the normal when the density is lower. And the sharper the change, the more the sound wave will be bent.

Sound waves are scattered by both the surface and the bottom of the ocean, and the arcs of their paths converge. This phenomenon is known as the convergence zone. A submarine in the convergence zone will not be detected even when the sonar transmitter is very close. A number of ships in World War II were lost to submarines lurking in the convergence zones.

The deep scattering layer also plays havoc with sonar. It is made up of a thick layer and sublayers made up of various kinds of plankton which reflect sound waves. Sound waves transmitted directly at the deep scattering layer sometimes will penetrate it, but the chances of penetration decrease sharply if the sound waves hit it at an angle. The deep scattering layer varies from area to area and by time of day in thickness, composition, and the depth at which it occurs.

When a sound wave enters the permanent thermocline, its velocity is drastically reduced. This layer of minimum velocity is known as the deep sound channel. It is theoretically possible for a submarine to operate in the deep sound channel without being detected by long-range sonar.

CHAPTER 9

"Room aboard for everything but a mistake"

A nuclear submarine is incredibly complex, wondrously sensitive, and awesomely powerful. It is also numbingly expensive. A Los Angeles-class fast attack submarine costs $750 million; a prototype of a new class may cost twice that much. And the gestation period of a prototype is long. First, the Navy decides what role a new class of submarines must fulfill, the weapons and sensors to be placed aboard, and the performance standards to be met. From that point to a finished prototype may take a decade.

Until the mid-1960s, submarines had one primary role: to attack enemy naval and merchant ships. That still is a primary role, but new roles have been added. Submarines capable of launching ballistic and cruise missiles now can strike directly at targets in the enemy's homeland. And submarines can locate and attack enemy submarines. Other submarine roles include general patrol duties and clandestine special operations. The particular role of a submarine determines its design.

Innovations incorporated into a new class have to be tested, not simply for individual performance but in relation to everything else on the submarine, because everything on a submarine affects everything else. Electric Boat says that a new submarine design requires

ENGINE ROOM

MISSILE
COMPARTMENT

MISSILE CONTROL
CENTER

608

CONTROL ROOM

REACTOR
COMPARTMENT

GYRO STABILIZER

WARDROOM

CREW'S QUARTERS

CREW'S
MESS

TORPEDO
ROOM

U.S.S. ETHAN ALLEN
SSB(N)608

**A cross section of the U.S.S.
Ethan Allen shows that most of
the available space is taken up
by the nuclear reactor and
engine room, missile compartment and control center, and
torpedo room.**

as many as two thousand working drawings. Blueprints from these drawings, if placed end to end, would make a strip 250 miles long. Finally, submarine construction involves some seven million parts, many of them unique in design and manufacture.

There is more science packed into a submarine than any other warship. To complicate matters, the space tolerances are infinitely more demanding. However, the Navy likes to say, "There is room for everything aboard a submarine except a mistake."

Design of a submarine involves four stages: inception, conceptual design, contract design, and working drawings. It starts in the Office of the Chief of Naval Operations (OPNAV), where the number and types of ships and submarines necessary to maintain an adequate naval force are determined. OPNAV proposes to the secretary of the Navy an annual shipbuilding program, usually involving both new construction and modernization of existing hulls. A request for a new submarine design originates in the Ship Characteristics Board of OPNAV.

Once a new design has been initiated, exploratory studies are made of available data and the performance characteristics are determined. Many design feasibility studies are made, and from these develops a set of tentative characteristics.

Then a set of drawings and data sheets is prepared showing the principal features of the basic design based on the approved submarine characteristics. During this stage the size and shape of the hull are determined. Models are tested to find a hull with the optimum maneuvering characteristics, the correct propeller design, and the shaft horsepower required.

This information is now checked, refined, and redrawn in greater detail. These are the contract drawings and ship specifications which become a part of the contract with the shipbuilder. The shipbuilder prepares the working drawings from which the submarine will be built.

Hull design is central to the submarine performance. At the end of World War II, the state of the art was the long, narrow, highly streamlined hull of the German Type XXI patrol submarine, and it was quickly adopted by the U.S., British, Russian, and French navies.

But as propulsion systems improved, control problems developed at speeds in excess of twelve knots. The submarine would begin to pitch to the point where, under certain conditions, control could be lost completely.

A breakthrough came in 1953, inspired by the aeronautical principles of the blimp. The new design was first used on the American diesel-electric experimental submarine *Albacore*. The shorter, fatter, more maneuverable hull was symmetrical along its long axis, like a torpedo.

The *Albacore* also incorporated sail planes, and was the first submarine that could "fly" like an airplane, making tightly banked curves and, reportedly, even underwater loops. The hull was stable at all speeds, and its 15,000 horsepower could drive it submerged at speeds in excess of thirty-three knots, unheard of at the time. The hull shape also provided greater internal storage space and a multideck layout. Most submarines in the free world now have a variation of the *Albacore* hull.

There are two overriding considerations in hull design: a submerged submarine must have neutral buoyancy, and a center of gravity lying below its center of buoyancy.

The center of buoyancy depends on the volume of water the submarine displaces, and is controlled by varying the volume of displacement. On the surface the main ballast tanks are filled with air; when submerged the tanks are filled with water. Filling the tanks with air moves the center of buoyancy above the center of gravity; the reverse

Powerful hydraulic lifts load torpedoes into the tubes in the torpedo room of the U.S.S. *John Adams.* Torpedoes now are secondary weapons aboard nuclear-powered ballistic missile submarines.

happens when the tanks are filled with water. The deeper a submarine dives, the greater the outside water pressure, and the pressure actually compresses the hull with a resulting loss of buoyancy of several tons.

Designers are increasingly concerned with the hull's metallurgy, thickness, and reenforcement, for these determine how deep a submarine can dive. Depth gives a submarine a greater margin of safety in high-speed maneuvers, and protection from detection.

Hydrodynamic efficiency is another factor. A submerged submarine is impeded by the total effect of three forms of drag: skin friction, form drag, and appendage drag. The *Albacore*'s hull greatly reduced skin friction, even with a cylindrical mid-body. Skin friction is directly proportional to surface area; the bigger the hull, the greater the drag.

Form drag accounts for only 2 to 4 percent of the total drag on an *Albacore* hull, but that's sufficient to concern the designers. Form drag is sharply increased by anything protruding from the hull, which is why the deck impedimenta of World War II submarines are gone. Built into the hull of a nuclear submarine are dozens of hatches, cleats, connections, and other items.

Streamlining has gone about as far as current research can take it, and designers now concentrate on the nature of the hull surface. Special paints can reduce friction, which means higher speeds. Speed also can be increased for short periods by releasing polymers around the hull.

Soviet designers cover the hulls of the Oscar-class submarines with tiles that are believed to provide acoustic absorption and boundary-layer pressure equalization. There have been reports that the Soviet developments came from studying dolphins and killer whales, whose skins help them adjust to boundary-layer pressure changes.

Marine mammal research may have led to fins or hydroplanes that change shape as the submarine's speed changes. The latest Soviet submarines have bulbous bows, shaped like the nose of a whale, and sails that resemble the fins of marine mammals.

Fins, or hydroplanes, are the major control surfaces of a submarine. The designer strives to attain the perfect compromise between maneuverability and low drag. The size, shape, and location of fins have changed over the years. The early Holland submarines had no forward hydroplanes; later submarines incorporated them to maintain an even keel in a dive. U.S. nuclear submarines have fins on their sails, but starting with the new *San Juan* they are gone, replaced by retractable hull fins.

Wherever the fins are placed, the submarine must meet critical maneuverability standards: turning within less than four times the submarine's length, and ascending and descending at rates of several hundred feet a minute.

The stern design also receives the close attention of the designers, particularly the correlation of hull shape, propeller, and control surfaces. During World War II the stern control surfaces were aft of the propeller. Most submarines now have horizontal control surfaces forward of the propeller. In a variation on this, Los Angeles- and Ohio-class nuclear submarines have vertical endplates on the aft horizontal fins, improving control and housing hydrophones.

Walrus-class Swedish and Dutch submarines incorporate X-shaped appendages which give greater operating control and are quieter. Whatever the placement, the complex relationship between steering and diving functions of the hydroplanes necessitates a computer-assisted operation.

To avoid enemy sonar a submarine must run quietly, but there are other design considerations in avoiding detection. A smaller submarine presents a smaller sonar target, but it takes a large submarine to house modern weapon and sensor systems. The hull can be shaped to diffuse sonar, but this can sharply increase drag. The sound-absorbing tiles now on Soviet submarines are the most promising development, and similar tiles will be incorporated in the next generation of American attack submarines.

There are four main types of hulls in use today: single hull, saddle tank, double hull, and multihull. Single-hull submarines have their main ballast tanks mounted within the hull itself or, as with the Los Angeles-class submarines, mounted externally at either end of the pressure hull. The main ballast tanks in saddle-tank submarines are mounted externally as additions to the pressure hull with free-flooding holes at the bottom and vents on the top. The British Navy uses saddle-tanks in its Oberon class.

Multihull submarines offer exceptional hull strength but are expensive and difficult to construct. Russian Typhoon-class ballistic-missile submarines reportedly have multihulls. Experts believe that these huge submarines have two complete, interconnected pressure

A crewman runs a systems check on one of the 16 missile tubes aboard the nuclear-powered submarine *Daniel Boone*. There are hundreds of systems aboard, and all are constantly monitored by the crew.

hulls, each with crew quarters and propulsion machinery; a third smaller section under the sail serves as the command and control center.

All submarine hulls are stiffened by ring frames and supported by traverse bulkheads. Both ends of the pressure hull have domed end-closures. All hulls, however, must have a ballast keel. The keel is mounted within the hull on double and multihull submarines, externally on single and saddle-tank hulls.

Hulls for American submarines are made of high-yield steel. Other countries have experimented with other materials: titanium, aluminum, even glass. Two classes of Russian submarines, Alfa and Mike, are built of titanium, stronger than steel and nonmagnetic. They cannot be detected by airborne MAD (Magnetic Airborne Detector) equipment or coils laid on the seabed. Titanium is exceedingly difficult to weld, but the Russian metallurgists apparently have mastered the technique.

Alfas are said to be capable of submerged speeds in excess of forty-two knots and can dive to somewhere between 2,000 and 3,000 feet, greater depths than any current American submarine can handle. The Soviets, who have poured billions into submarine research, refer to the Alfa as the "Golden Fish."

All current American nuclear-powered submarines use a pressurized-water reactor to superheat water under high pressure to prevent it from boiling, and send it to a steam generator. Heat energy is transferred in the generator from the superheated water in the primary circuit to unpressurized water in the secondary circuit. This produces steam, which is passed to the turbine. After driving the turbine, the steam goes into a series of condensers where it becomes water and is returned to the steam generator for recycling.

A constant flow of seawater is used by condensers for cooling. This is provided mechanically if the submarine is under way at speed; pumps are used under other conditions. But the pumps are noisy. In search of a quieter system, designers have tested alternative coolants. The *Seawolf* was fitted in the late 1950s with a liquid-sodium-cooled reactor. This gave excellent heat transference, but had service problems. If the sodium wasn't kept constantly heated, it solidified and ruined the primary circuit pipes. The plant was plagued with steam leaks, and finally was replaced by a water-cooled system.

The Russians seem to have better luck with liquid-metal cooling systems. Alfa-class submarines reportedly use a liquid-metal-cooled reactor. Alfas also have unmanned, automated engine rooms, cutting the amount of reactor shielding needed.

Modern propellers have as many as seven blades, which run at a very low number of revolutions per minute. Despite design refinements, propellers are a major source of noise, and each propeller design produces a unique sound. The nationality and class of a submarine can be identified by sophisticated sonar devices from its characteristic sound "signature."

A view of the second level of the missile compartment on an Ohio-class submarine. The largest American submarines, they are 560 feet long, weigh 18,750 tons submerged, and carry a crew of 160.

Whatever the refinements, the noise problem cannot be entirely eliminated; a moving submarine creates some noise and leaves a wake. In the wake are thermal and ultraviolet radiation disruptions and trails of dying microorganisms, all of which can be detected by sophisticated sensors.

A submarine-launched cruise missile (SLCM) is a pilotless aircraft propelled by an air-breathing engine that operates aerodynamically within the earth's atmosphere. In flight a cruise missile is controlled and guided, either by an on-board computer or remotely by satellite.

A submarine-launched ballistic missile (SLBM), however, is a rocket, propelled into space by one or more boosters. The thrust is terminated at an early stage, and the missile follows a trajectory that is governed by gravity and aerodynamic drag, although minor corrections can be made in flight.

Ballistic missiles can carry a greater payload over a much greater distance than can a cruise missile, but they sacrifice pinpoint accuracy and total control. A cruise missile, for example, can fly close to

A Poseidon missile (PEM-4) roars skyward a split second after being launched from the submerged fleet ballistic submarine U.S.S. *Daniel Boone.* The submarine's antenna is seen to the right.

the ground, hugging the terrain to avoid radar detection.

The first cruise missiles aboard submarines were launched through torpedo tubes. These included the Sub-Harpoon antiship missile and the Tomahawk, which could attack both ships and land targets. The Navy then decided that the missiles took up too much space in the torpedo room, and they were placed in vertically mounted launching tubes between the bow sonar and the forward end of the pressure hull. The SM39 Exocet, a French antiship missile fired from torpedo tubes, proved effective in the 1982 Falkland Islands war.

In the 1950s the U.S. Navy introduced carrier-based AJ-1 Savages, capable of carrying the Mark V atomic bomb. This spurred the Soviets to begin a crash program to build attack and cruise missile submarines.

In the last months of World War II the Germans were considering using submarines to launch V-2 rockets against American targets. Nazi submarine and rocket technology helped both the U.S. and Russia advance the concept of a ballistic missile submarine. The Soviet Navy was first. Diesel-powered submarines armed with three SS-N-3 missiles came into service in 1958. Crude by today's standards, a submarine had to surface to launch missiles.

The U.S. Navy countered with Polaris, a dramatic breakthrough in missile system technology. Developed by Admiral W. F. Rayborn and Lockheed, the Polaris met its two initial requirements: the use of a solid propellant and the capability of underwater launching. Also incorporated in the Polaris system: lightweight reentry vehicles, miniaturized inertial guidance, miniaturized nuclear and thermo-

At the big American submarine facility in Holy Loch, Scotland, a crane on the submarine tender U.S.S. *Hunley* off-loads a Polaris missile from the U.S.S. *Thomas A. Edison.* Work at Holy Loch goes on around the clock.

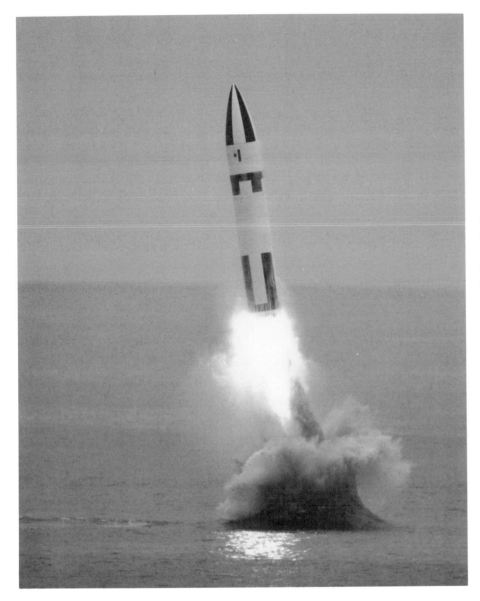

A Polaris A-3 is launched from
a submerged submarine. The
first of the Navy's missiles, the
Polaris has given way to the
more accurate, longer-ranged
Poseidon and the Trident C-4
and D-5.

nuclear warheads, cold-gas launch techniques, and submarine inertial navigation. When the Polaris system went into service in November
1960, it changed the entire nature of strategic warfare.

The Soviets weren't long in catching up. A new missile, the
SS-N-5, could be launched from a submerged submarine, and the
SS-N-6 was small enough for a Yankee-class submarine to carry sixteen. This brought parity with U.S. ballistic submarines. The SS-N-
8 missile had a range of 4,800 nautical miles, by far the longest at
that time. The next development, the SS-N-9, gave the Soviet Navy
a multiple, independently targetable, reentry vehicle (MIRV).

Another major Soviet advancement was the SS-N-18, a missile with
a range of 4,300 nautical miles. The U.S. didn't match it until the
Trident II became operational ten years later. The latest Soviet missiles are the SS-N-20 and SS-N-23, both with ranges of 4,800 nautical

miles, and carried by Typhoon and Delta IV submarines.

The submarine is a mobile launch pad, but in order for a missile launch to be effective, the captain needs to know the precise position, velocity, and depth of his submarine. The navigation system transmits this data continuously to fire control. Inertial navigation (SINS) records every movement of the submarine in relation to a theoretical stable platform, and can be updated with input from LORAN or optical observations.

Fire control prepares and fires the missiles. It sets up the missile guidance system inertial platform, determines true launch bearing, stores and computes target data, and passes data to the missile guidance computer.

The launch system stores, protects, and ejects the missiles, which are enclosed in capsules stowed inside shock-protected, watertight launch tubes. Some missiles are ejected by compressed air, others by steam.

About ninety feet after the missile clears the tube, the first-stage motor ignites to propel the missile through the ocean surface, into the atmosphere, and up into space. When the first stage has been expended, it separates and falls away, and the second-stage motor ignites and propels the missile. The Trident and the Soviet SS-N-20 and SS-N-23 missiles have a third-stage motor.

The missile's navigation equipment continuously measures linear acceleration from its inertial system, altering the missile's trajectory to counteract any outside forces such as wind that affect acceleration. When the missile arrives at the correct velocity, altitude, and position for the target, the bus carrying the reentry vehicles (RVs) separates from the final stage and continues its flight. Individual RVs are dropped off according to instructions fed into the missile's computer just before the launch. The warheads reenter the atmosphere at steep angles, a special coating absorbing the heat. Decoys are released with the warheads to deceive antimissile systems.

The first SLBMs had a single reentry vehicle containing the warhead. Advanced technology led to multiple-reentry vehicles (MRVs). The warheads were all aimed at the same target, but were spread out in a shotgun pattern. The next step was the development of independently targetable reentry vehicles (MIRVs), which could be dropped off the reentry vehicle at different points to hit individual targets. State-of-the-art missiles now incorporate maneuverable reentry vehicles (MARVs), which can steer precisely to the target independent of the accuracy of the launch.

Warhead accuracy is measured in terms of "circular area probable" (cep). This is the radius of a circle centered on the point of aim into which 50 percent of all warheads launched can be expected to hit. The first SLBMs were reasonably inaccurate because they were totally dependent on the submarine's SINS, but there has been steady improvement. Polaris had a cep of 0.5 nautical miles; Poseidon, 0.3; Trident I, 0.23. That means a submarine can launch a Trident missile at a target nearly five thousand miles away and half of the war-heads will hit within some five hundred yards of dead center.

The Soviet SS-N 20 missile, however, has a range 750 miles longer and is nearly as accurate with a cep of 0.35.

The increasing degree of accuracy of ballistic missiles has brought about a change in defense planning. The early missiles were limited to area targets, such as cities and large military installations. But the newer MARV missiles, capable of accuracy measured in tens of feet, could be effective against such small targets as enemy missile silos. The comparative accuracy of competitors' ballistic missiles has a profound effect on the balance of power.

Trident I carries a similar payload to that of the Poseidon but with a much greater range, 4,230 nautical miles compared to Poseidon's 2,500. This permits a much larger area of operations. Trident I owes its increased range to an aerospike on the nose of the missile, which reduces drag by 50 percent; to improved fuel; and to a third-stage motor.

Trident II was designed for greater accuracy, and the nearly 46-foot missile can carry fourteen RVs, although the SALT II agreement imposes an RV limit of ten. Twenty Ohio-class submarines reportedly will each carry twenty Trident IIs. Four British submarines also are receiving Trident IIs.

In the age of missiles, torpedoes still are an important part of a submarine's arsenal. They have been modernized in an attempt to meet the new standards of naval warfare. Torpedo speed is a problem. The U.S. Mark 46 torpedo travels at forty knots, but so does a Soviet Alfa-class submarine, which eliminates the possibility of a stern shot. A program called Advanced Capability (ADCAP) reportedly will raise the speed of the Mark 48 torpedo to fifty-five knots.

Great progress has been made in torpedo guidance systems. Torpedoes now incorporate a sonar transducer that switches from passive to active automatically once the target responds to the attack. Guidance wires link the torpedo to the submarine and can both control the torpedo and pass sonar information to the submarine's fire-control system.

Stronger-hulled submarines, such as the double-hulled Soviet Typhoon class, have necessitated greater explosive power in the torpedo's warhead. Directed-energy torpedo warheads also are effective.

But the torpedo still is far from being a perfect weapon. In the Falkland Islands war, both the British and the Argentinian navies reported numerous instances of malfunctioning torpedoes. It is ironic that while the Whitehead torpedo was developed before there was a submarine capable of launching it, torpedoes now trail submarines in performance.

Submarines still lay mines, now launching them from their torpedo tubes. Planes, helicopters, and surface ships also lay mines, but submarines excel when the mines need to be laid secretly and precisely. Conversely, modern mines are effective antisubmarine weapons,

Workers in a missile tube aboard the ballistic submarine *James Madison* suggest the awesome size of the Trident missiles that can fly with deadly accuracy to a target thousands of miles away.

A canister container is used to load Trident missiles aboard an Ohio-class submarine. Each of the 24 Tridents is 44 feet long and 83 inches in diameter, weighs nearly 60 tons, and carries 8 warheads.

triggering on a submarine's acoustic, magnetic, or electrical signature. Particularly lethal is the U.S. Navy's Captor (enCAPsulated TORpedo), which lies on the bottom and fires a torpedo.

A submerged submarine is blind, totally dependent on its sensors, particularly its sonar. SSNs and SSBNs have a large sonar mounted in the bow and, just aft, large arrays of conformal sonar. Underwater listening devices called hydrophones are on the bow, amidships, and near the stern. Among other things, the hull hydrophones monitor the submarine's own noises. When a submarine leaves port, a surface ship checks its noise level, but new noises can develop at sea. If undetected, they can attract the enemy.

Active sonar devices transmit acoustic pulses at audio frequency levels at a rate that ranges from 12.5 to 700 milliseconds, depending on oceanic conditions. Highly sophisticated equipment assists sonar operators in assimilating and processing the sonar signals. Large numbers of transducers mounted in arrays make up active sonar systems. In the bow, cylindrical arrays electronically form a beam giving directional resolution. A shift in the return signal indicates a moving target.

Missile tubes gape open ready
for loading with Trident C-4
missiles aboard the U.S.S. *Ohio*.
Ballistic submarines have a
destructive firepower capacity
never dreamt of a few decades
ago.

Several problems are inherent in active sonar: noise generated by the parent submarine is picked up along with incoming signals; changing oceanic conditions often distort the beams; and sonar signals can be picked up by enemy sonar.

Los Angeles-class submarines carry the BQQ-5 active sonar system spherically mounted in their bows. This system employs the Submarine Active Detection System (SADS) and is integrated with other systems on board, including the Mine Detection Avoidance Sonar (MIDAS) and systems to enable the submarine to operate beneath the polar ice cap.

Current sonar research focuses on increasing its ability to detect, while reducing its revealing signature. One development is spread-spectrum transmission in which the signal is varied over a preprogrammed transmission band, reducing the chance of the enemy picking it out of the background of oceanic noises.

Passive sonar, involving no transmission, no chance of betraying the submarine's position, is precisely tuned to pick up submarine and ship signatures through hydrophones. The signals are processed by powerful computers and analyzed by specialists. The U.S. Navy has a clear lead in this arcane science.

Passive sonars usually use the same arrays as the active sonar system. Towed arrays often are employed, comprising as many as several hundred hydrophones. Los Angeles-class SSNs use the BQQ-25, a towed array with a 2,624-foot cable. One advantage of a towed array is its unique ability to scan rearward. This is countered by several disadvantages: the submarine must slow down and run in a straight line while operating a towed array, and its size makes it a problem to store on-board. Soviet submarines also use a variety of towed arrays.

Once, the submarine's only sensor was its periscope. Submarines now normally have two, one for general use and a smaller one employed while attacking surface ships. The modern periscope is a highly sophisticated instrument capable of many tasks. Among its equipment: a microprocessor to estimate bearing and range and to feed the information into the fire-control system; a laser rangefinder accurate to within three feet; artificial horizon sextants to take quick sights to update the submarine's inertial navigational system; sensors to warn of electronic threats; thermal imagers for night or bad-weather use; and still and television cameras.

Like everything else aboard a submarine, the periscopes involve compromises. To use his periscopes, a commander must put his submarine in a dangerous position. The exposed part of the periscope makes a wake that can be seen or picked up by radar. At speeds above ten knots, the periscope vibrates, and the longer the tube, the greater the vibration. But a short tube brings the submarine that much closer to the surface and its attendant perils.

Other sensors poke out of a submarine's sail. There are radio direction-finding antennas and radar to search the sea and sky. Adding in air intakes and the antennas for various communication equipment, a Los Angeles-class submarine has twelve masts. When the submarine submerges, the masts retract into the sail and are covered by

A lieutenant looks through the periscope of the nuclear-powered ballistic missile submarine U.S.S. *Ohio* during precommissioning sea trials. Special goggles increase the officer's night vision.

remotely controlled hatches, reducing turbulence and noise.

Through World War II a submarine had to surface to use its radio. There was no way to communicate with a submerged submarine, but a submarine couldn't stay submerged for very long anyway. Today's submarines can stay submerged for months at a time, and surfacing involves the risk of detection. This has spurred developments in radio technology.

Radio waves are weakened as they pass through water, and the higher the frequency, the greater the loss in strength. And radio waves, like sound waves, are distorted underwater.

Radio signals of very low frequency (3kHz to 30kHz) can reach a submarine fifty feet below the surface. To receive VLF broadcasts, a submarine will either trail a long wire antenna, or a loop antenna mounted on a buoy. The problem is that letting out the wire or buoy creates noise.

The U.S. Navy has seven shore-based VLF transmitting stations, NATO two, and Britain one. The Soviets have ten. The antennas for VLF stations are big, expensive, and vulnerable to attack.

A further development is radio communication at extremely low frequencies (300Hz to 3kHz), which can be received by a submarine at 500 feet. Innovative new equipment reportedly can transmit successfully to 1,300 feet. ELF, as this is called, is practically impervious to either jamming or the effects of a nuclear explosion, which makes it particularly suited for communicating with second-strike SSBNs.

However, the information transmission rate is extremely low. The U.S. Navy's Austere ELF system reportedly takes fifteen minutes to transmit a three-letter group, although highly compressed codes make it possible to send a lot of information using three-letter groups. ELF systems also need huge transmitting antennas.

The U.S. Navy set up a test facility more than a decade ago at Clam Lake, Wisconsin, which used telephone poles to support an X-shaped antenna with arms seven miles long. Transmitting at a power of only two watts, it was able to reach a submarine 427 feet beneath 33 feet of Arctic ice. The Clam Lake facility now is used in conjunction with a similar installation at K. I. Sawyer Air Force base in Michigan to provide a full operation system.

The primary means of communicating with fleet submarines now is the TACAMO (Take Charge and Move Out) system. Two squadrons of Lockheed EC-130AQ aircraft, one in the Atlantic, one in the Pacific, act as radio relays between the command and the SSBNs. One aircraft is over each ocean at any given time, and another is on fifteen-minutes notice on the ground.

The planes have a communications center with a variety of equipment that can transmit in VLF, LF, HF, and UHF bands. To transmit on VLF, a wire antenna more than six miles long is trailed from the aircraft. A new plane, the E-6, is taking over the TACAMO system. Fifteen E-6s were on order in 1990 at a total cost of two billion dollars.

Buoys of various types are used as relays in communicating with submerged submarines. The SSQ-86 (XN-1) is a down-link communication (DCL) buoy that transmits a programmed message to a submarine without requiring the submarine to reveal its position.

The DCL is mounted in a standard sonobuoy and can be launched from an aircraft or surface ship. The buoy transmits its message (limited to four groups of three characters) once near the surface, descends to a predetermined depth, transmits a second time, pauses for five minutes, transmits a third time, then self-destructs. The entire process takes some seventeen minutes.

Laser has a potential for communicating with submarines. There is an optical window in the blue-green part of the spectrum that allows laser transmissions to penetrate to considerable depths. Considerable power is needed, for such transmissions and satellites can't carry the necessary generating equipment. A way around this is to use a laser on the ground to bounce the signal off a space-based mirror. This way, transmissions could be made three hundred times faster than with an ELF system, although the receiving submarine would have to be closer to the surface.

Submarines can run at periscope depth, using a mast-mounted antenna to beam messages off satellites. Such transmissions are hard to detect from ground monitoring stations, although they can be detected by aircraft with special detection equipment, and by other satellites.

Transmitting buoys, such as the U.S. Navy's BRT-1, can relay messages from a submarine to bases on shore or to surface ships. The buoy can be preset to delay the transmission from fifteen minutes to an hour, permitting the submarine to clear the area, lessening the chance of detection.

It is exceptionally difficult for one submerged submarine to communicate with another. Under certain circumstances acoustic underwater telephones can be used, but usually intercommunication between submarines involves sending the message to the base to be relayed to the other submarine by one of the various communication channels.

Communication technology continually improves, but a ballistic submarine still must often operate on its own, completely out of touch for long periods of time from its command, other submarines, and surface ships and aircraft. Although he cannot fire missiles unless ordered to do so, the commander must make many combat decisions himself.

CHAPTER 10

"The United States no longer has mastery of the seas"

Ballistic submarine bases are, by necessity, large, and their locations cannot be kept secret. The U.S. has three—Kings Bay, Georgia; Bangor, Washington; and Holy Loch, Scotland—to support, maintain, repair, and refit SSBNs and their missiles, and to provide necessary services to their crews.

The oldest base is Holy Loch. President Eisenhower met with Prime Minister Sir Anthony Douglas-Home in the early 1950s and negotiated permission to establish a submarine repair facility in British waters to replace the submarine facility at Rota, Spain. Holy Loch, just north of Glasgow, was selected because it provided easy access to the strategic waters of the eastern Atlantic.

The submarine tender *Proteus* and a Polaris missile support ship took up residence at Holy Loch early in 1961. By 1985 Holy Loch was a large base with a floating dry dock and the headquarters of Commander Submarine Squadron 14. More than six hundred patrols have sailed from the base, which is designated Site 1 Holy Loch. Site 1 is the abbreviated name of the U.S. Navy's Fleet Ballistic Submarine Refit Site 1, and some 1,600 Navy personnel are stationed there.

Holy Loch has been described as an "industrial Las Vegas, available to 'customers' twenty-four hours a day, 365 days a year." The base averages 23 refits and some 9,400 repairs annually. A saying at Holy Loch: "We can fix everything over here except the crack of dawn."

The next base was Bangor, the 6,929-acre site of a former torpedo station annex on Puget Sound. Construction began in late 1974 and was completed a decade later. The base has nearly five thousand military personnel and employs some three thousand civilians. Bangor houses several commands: Naval Submarine Base, Trident Refit Facility, Trident Training Facility, and Strategic Weapons Facility, Pacific.

An officer stationed at Bangor says, "For the first time, if a man really wants to, he can put in almost an entire Navy career here. He could complete a three-year submarine tour and then come ashore at one of a number of Trident activities on base, or serve at the nearby Keyport Torpedo Station, or the Puget Sound Naval Shipyard in Bremerton. If the sailor likes it here, he can put down some real roots and become an active member of the community. I think we're going to have a more stable Navy because of people who elect to do things like that."

The naval bases at New London, Connecticut, and Charleston, South Carolina, service fast attack submarines and the earlier SSBNs but can't accommodate Ohio-class Tridents. In anticipation of this problem, the Navy decided to expand its facilities at Kings Bay, near Savannah on the Georgia coast. In 1980 it was designated the Atlantic base for Trident submarines, and became fully operational late in 1989. Kings Bay is the home base for Submarine Squadron 16. Like Bangor, Kings Bay contains training and refit facilities.

Rescue ships like the U.S.S. *Sunbird* carry equipment and divers to assist submarines in trouble. Nuclear submarines dive much deeper than do diesel submarines, making rescue operations more difficult.

Everything at these bases is geared to the schedule of the Tridents: a 75-day deployment followed by a 25-day refit period, one week of which is taken up by the blue-gold crew changeover. This allows base personnel only eighteen days for all refit work. Meeting this tight schedule requires round-the-clock work seven days a week.

Good management and reliable equipment at these facilities enable the Navy to keep 65 percent of its Trident submarines at sea at all times, an improvement on the 45 percent for earlier classes. By contrast, the Soviet Navy with more SSBNs is only able to keep 13 percent of them on patrol at the same time.

Under a NATO commitment, the French have two SSBNs constantly on patrol, the British, one. NATO's SSBNs are operated by three different navies under three separate national controls, the U.S., Britain, and France. Each country retains control over its own SLBM warheads.

If the Soviet Union should attack Western Europe, it would face a nuclear submarine force. Britain and France, individually or in concert, could inflict a destructive retaliatory attack on Soviet land. The British SSBNs are based at Faslane, on the Gare Loch off the River Clyde in Scotland, the French at Brest.

SSBN bases are impossible to hide, and submarine arrivals and departures are closely monitored by satellite and other electronic devices. British SSBNs go to sea in full view of anyone who cares to watch through the narrows at Rhu just north of Helensburgh; the French have a similar situation at Brest. Such narrows are called choke points by submariners, and they have a strategic importance.

After passing a choke point a submarine going on or coming in from patrol is easily detectable by satellite in the relatively shallow waters of the continental shelf. Once clear of the shelf, though, an SSBN dives deep and travels at top speed to its patrol area, making sure that it isn't being followed by enemy SSNs. On station, an SSBN will cruise at about three knots, varying its depth to match prevailing oceanic conditions to find the convergence zone where it is safe from enemy sonar. However, it risks detection when it rises near the surface to communicate or update its inertial navigation system.

The Soviet Navy understandably regards its ballistic missile fleet as its most valuable asset, and the U.S. Navy's fleet as a major threat. Military observers believe that the Soviet surface fleet was designed primarily to protect the SSBN fleet, although independent forays may be a secondary capability. As evidence of this, the Soviet Navy didn't have an aircraft carrier until a few years ago.

Early Soviet SSBNs, the Yankee class, patrolled close to the coast of the United States because their missiles had a limited range. In October 1986 a missile exploded aboard a Yankee, forcing it to surface some 750 nautical miles from Washington, D.C. The 1,600-nautical-mile range of the missiles aboard the Yankees enabled them to threaten such targets as the East Coast Strategic Air Command bases.

In the Far East, Soviet SSBNs concentrate in the Sea of Okhotsk;

French Agosta-class diesel-powered attack submarines were developed in the 1970s to carry conventional and wire-guided torpedoes. A UN embargo stopped South Africa from buying two Agostas.

Entering port with her crew on deck is the French nuclear-powered ballistic missile submarine *L'Indomptable.* French and British submarines are independent strike forces under NATO control.

to the west, in the Barents Sea. This compels the U.S. Navy and its allies to send submarines, surface ships, and antisubmarine aircraft to these areas. The Soviet SSBN base at Polyarnyi on the Kola Peninsula apparently is too small for Typhoon-class submarines but handles Yankees and Deltas. A new base with protective pens is said to be nearing ready at Gremikha. Soviet SSBNs in the Far East are based at Vladivostok and at Petropavlovsk on the Kamchatka Peninsula.

Submarines operating out of Vladivostok have a choke point in the Kunashir Passage to the north of Japan. The Soviet Baltic fleet has a choke point between the Danish island of Zealand and the Swedish coast.

In the Mediterranean, where the Soviets usually have up to eight submarines, the choke points are the Bosporus, around the Aegean Islands, in the Aegean Straits of Kíthira and Kárpathos, in the Sicilian Channel, and in the Straits of Gibraltar.

One of the most dramatic developments of the post–World War II period has been the growth of Soviet naval strength. From the end of the war until the early 1970s, the United States maintained unquestioned naval supremacy. This gave great flexibility to American foreign policy and provided one of the West's primary shields against Soviet aggression. Today, however, the Soviet Union is a true sea power, challenging the United States in all aspects of maritime activity.

The Soviet Navy concentrated on building up its submarine force in the belief that it could achieve strategic goals in war at sea despite constantly improving antisubmarine weapons. Submarines also were a relatively inexpensive and rapid means of increasing Soviet naval power. From 1945 to 1955 more than 450 diesel attack submarines were built; then the Soviets concentrated on nuclear-powered submarines. Some were flawed and unsafe, but they were the technological beginning upon which is built the Soviet Union's current fleet of nearly two hundred nuclear submarines.

The Soviet submarine program was described in a 1988 U.S. Department of Defense report, *Soviet Military Power: An Assessment of the Threat,* as "the world's largest strategic missile submarine force" with the majority of its submarines armed with intercontinental-range missiles "that can reach North America from Soviet ports and coastal waters."

Valiants, the first nuclear submarine class of exclusively British design, usually operate in close support of a task force or convoy, unlike U.S. attack submarines, which patrol independently.

Clockwise from opposite page:

**Diesel-powered Tango-class
attack submarines armed with
antisubmarine missiles are in
service in the Soviet fleet. The
Soviets have seven classes of
submarines in production, the
U.S. has two.**

**A Soviet Yankee-class subma-
rine armed with seven missiles
runs on the surface near the
East Coast of the U.S. This class
has a second-strike mission,
probably to attack U.S. ports
and airfields.**

**After colliding with a merchant
ship, a damaged Soviet Victor-
class submarine is aided by a
tender. It carries a special torpedo that is believed to automatically home in on a ship
wake.**

**The Mike-class, used to test
developments in propulsion, is
one of three current classes of
Soviet attack submarines. The
high cost of Russia's submarine
program has undermined the
country's economy.**

The Soviet naval policy was summed up succinctly in the late 1980s by S. G. Gorshkov, Admiral of the Fleet of the Soviet Union and full member of the Central Committee of the Communist Party: "The flag of the Soviet Navy flies over the oceans of the world. Sooner or later the United States will have to understand it no longer has mastery of the seas."

The U.S. Navy's submarine fleet currently is armed with a mix of Poseidon and Trident missiles. The Navy does not discuss the SSBN patrol areas, but certain assumptions can be made. The range of the Trident permits submarines to patrol in the Atlantic, Pacific, and Indian oceans and under the polar ice cap. By staying near the maximum range, the SSBNs still threaten the major industrial and population centers of the U.S.S.R., both European and Far Eastern, while making Soviet antisubmarine warfare more difficult.

The ninth and tenth Trident submarines, the *Tennessee* and the *West Virginia,* carry Trident II (D-5) missiles. The Navy plans to add one Trident a year equipped with D-5 missiles. Older Tridents will be modified to the D-5s. The older Poseidon SSBNs will begin to be phased out within the next decade. By the end of the century, the SSBN force will be composed entirely of quieter, more capable Trident SSBNs armed with D-5 missiles. This program has a price tag in excess of twenty billion dollars.

SSBNs have a single mission: to threaten the enemy's homeland with their ballistic missiles. Attack submarines are much more flexible and have a variety of missions. They are armed with torpedoes and / or cruise missiles, and can attack enemy submarines, surface ships, and land targets. They escort SSBNs going out or coming in from patrol. They patrol the choke points through which enemy submarines must pass. They keep sea lanes clear for task groups or convoys. They pursue hostile SSBNs and other targets. And they conduct general searches of the ocean.

A fast attack submarine often will operate at very low speeds, using only its passive sonar until enemy contact is made. Active sonar would be used briefly, perhaps only a single pulse, to confirm the target's range and bearing. Even that would be enough to alert the target, but would not give away the attack submarine's position. Should the search area prove free of the enemy, the attack submarine will proceed to another search area at top speed to minimize the time period in which it is at risk of being detected.

Submarines are ideal for clandestine operations because they can approach hostile shores unseen. They deliver mines, miniature submarines or submersibles, or small landing parties with equal ease. In World War II, submarines were used to deliver supplies to guerrillas, and to land and pick up raiding parties.

The *Nautilus* and the converted mine layer *Argonaut* delivered more than two hundred U.S. Marines to Makin Island in the Gilberts in 1942, where they destroyed a seaplane base. The next year the *Nautilus* and the *Narwhal* delivered a raiding party to Attu in the Aleu-

tians. The British also used submarines for clandestine operations
on the coast of Nazi-occupied Europe.

The Axis also made imaginative use of their submarines. The Italian Navy used them to take miniature submarines and frogmen to
enemy bases. Italian miniature submarines in World War II sank or
severely damaged 63,000 tons of Allied warships and 50,000 tons of
merchant shipping. A German submarine landed trained saboteurs
on the eastern tip of Long Island in a famous incident of the war.

Diesel-powered submarines are particularly well suited for clandestine operations because they run more quietly underwater than
do nuclear submarines. A Soviet Whiskey-class diesel submarine,
apparently on a clandestine mission, ran aground in 1981 off the
Swedish naval base at Karlskrona.

The Soviet Navy has special units called Spetsnaz to carry out
clandestine operations off submarimes. A Spetsnaz unit used a miniature submarine to reconnoiter Swedish naval bases in the Stockholm archipelago in October 1982. With an uncharacteristic bit of
humor, a photograph of one of the Soviet miniature submarines was
published in *Pravda* in the mid-1970s with the explanation that such
vessels would be used to search for the lost city of Atlantis.

Less amusing is the possibility that Soviet miniature submarines
might be used to lay nuclear mines at the exit points from U.S. and
NATO submarine bases, or to interfere with such NATO seabed
installations as the SOSUS sonar network.

The U.S. Navy has two special forces: Underwater Demolition Teams
(UDT) and Sea-Air-Land (SEAL) teams. In World War II, UDTs cleared
landing areas of mines and other obstructions, performed beach
reconnaissance missions, and destroyed specific targets such as roads
and bridges.

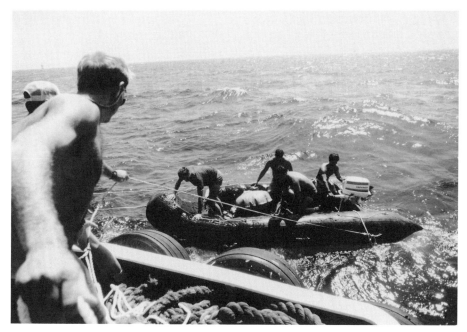

In the Gulf of Suez, explosive
ordnance divers aboard a rubber raft participate in a Navy
mine countermeasure operation.
Mine clearance is an essential
part of thwarting enemy antisubmarine measures.

SEAL teams are made up of UDT members who have been combat-trained to operate in hostile territory. A SEAL team is made up of 27 officers and 156 enlisted men comprising five platoons, each capable of independent operations: reconnaissance, demolition, and sabotage. A SEAL team might be used, for example, to destroy an enemy SSBN base.

Several U.S. submarines have been converted to carry SEAL teams. The attack submarine *Grayback* was converted in 1967 to carry seven officers and sixty men and their specialized equipment. The *Grayback* operated out of the Subic Bay naval base in the Philippines. Two Ethan Allen-class nuclear-powered SSBNs, the *Sam Houston* and the *John Marshall,* later were converted to SEAL team carriers, greatly extending the range of possible clandestine operations.

Most antisubmarine engagements involve five stages: search, contact, approach, close combat, and disengagement. Sometimes the search is general, part of the protective measures for a convoy, say, or is dictated by information gained from SOSUS or satellites.

The search stage is carried out by what the Navy calls the hunting platform—surface warship, submarine, or aircraft—following a general search pattern, or as part of a task force patrolling a designated area. Like the submarine it seeks, the hunting platform wants to avoid detection and usually will employ passive sonar.

Detection and classification are both part of the contact stage. Once a possible target is discovered in the search area, the platform determines its speed and bearing, then whether it is really a submarine and not a merchant ship or a school of fish. The contact's acoustic signature is fed into the platform's computer. State-of-the-art equipment can determine from the acoustic signature the type, class, and sometimes even the individual submarine.

A swimmer delivery vehicle is carefully loaded aboard the submarine U.S.S. *Grayback* under the supervision of members of a SEAL team at the U.S. submarine base at Subic Bay, the Philippines.

Now the platform begins the approach stage, tracking the target with passive sonar as it maneuvers into position to attack.

To attack, the hunter must be in a position to launch its weapons with reasonable certainty that they will hit the target. The weapon that is most risky is the torpedo, even though most modern torpedoes are equipped with sensors and wire-guidance links back to the launcher. Submarines attempt to compensate for torpedo unreliability by firing at targets at only half the torpedo's effective range of ten to twelve nautical miles.

If the first attack fails, the hunter and its target enter into close combat, each trying to destroy the other. Close combat between two submarines is the underwater equivalent of an aerial dogfight, and the performance capabilities of the individual submarine often is the determining factor.

After the battle comes disengagement, and usually a resumption of the search stage.

Denying the enemy the effective use of his submarines is the purpose of antisubmarine warfare, and this often can be accomplished without destroying them. This phase of naval warfare, the neutralization of enemy submarines, has the highest priority and commands a major portion of the naval budget.

The fast attack submarine operates deep enough to take advantage of the ambient conditions of the ocean to avoid detection. It can spend long periods at sea. Its detection systems are capable of locating targets at considerable distances; its weapons can destroy targets with minimum risk to itself.

All this has made the attack submarine a difficult target for enemy surface ships. As a result, the most effective weapon against an attack submarine is another attack submarine. Yet surface task forces must be able to mount their own antisubmarine-warfare operations.

Surface antisubmarine warfare involves two basic situations, the defense of naval vessels and the protection of merchantmen. Military experts assume that in a future war the areas of naval conflict are apt to be the major shipping lanes of the North Atlantic, and the Norwegian Sea, the Baltic, and the Mediterranean. On the other side of the world, the probable areas are the north and central Pacific.

To protect a large task force, three antisubmarine zones are formed. In the inner protection zone, warships and helicopters use active sonar to make sure the area is free of enemy submarines. Within this area, normally about sixty square miles, ships maneuver constantly to make it difficult for an attacking submarine to set up its weapons. The ships use hull-mounted sonar and may tow noisemakers to decoy a possible acoustic torpedo attack.

The middle zone is patrolled by ships and aircraft employing passive sonar. Ships use towed arrays, and helicopters use sonobuoys, allowing them to patrol a larger area than by dunking sonars.

The outer zone is in advance of the task force. Here long-range marine patrol (LRMP) aircraft such as the P-3 Orion and the S-3

A SH-3S Sea King lowers its sonar dome during an antisubmarine exercise. Helicopters are also used to hover over a submerged submarine and exchange radio messages free from interception.

Viking bring to bear the full panoply of detection systems, including radar, directional and nondirectional sonobuoys, and magnetic anomaly detector (MAD) equipment. Data from these systems is fed into the on-board computer. The aircraft are armed with torpedoes, missiles, and depth charges to attack any enemy submarine they locate.

On the edges of the outer zone are the fast attack submarines, the hunter-killers, using their speed to cover large areas. These submarines operate on the assumption that anything they encounter is the enemy.

The constant zigzagging of its ships forces the task force to move slowly, probably not more than ten knots. The task force commander is in constant communication with the antisubmarine forces. He also receives information from satellite surveillance.

Should an enemy submarine be detected, it can be attacked by a variety of weapons, depending on how far the submarine is from the task force. A submarine more than five miles away would be attacked by helicopters using homing torpedoes and by frigates and destroyers released from their sectors to form an independent attack unit. These ships also would launch their own helicopters armed with torpedoes.

But positive sonar contact with a submarine is exceedingly difficult to establish. Ships often will search in vain for hours; the initial detection may have been in error or the submarine realized it had been detected and fled.

One of the responsibilities of the force commander is to respond to a detected submarine. He can change course to move away from the danger area, but to do this every time may critically delay his mission. To frame the appropriate response, he establishes theoretical danger zones around the task force; the degree of danger inherent in each zone dictates the antisubmarine response.

The criteria for assessing potential threats involve what are called the limiting lines of submerged approach. They take into consideration the location of the submarine in relation to the task force, the speeds of each, and if and when the submarine can get in position to attack. In World War II these lines were entered by hand as overlays on plotting tables; today they are generated by computer and flashed on the commander's attack information screen. This data doesn't relieve the commander from making a judgment call, but it does help him weigh the risks.

The defense of merchant shipping is vital in the event of war. More than 99 percent of world trade still is carried by ship. Some thirty million tons of crude oil are delivered every day to Western Europe and America, most of it from the Middle East. Military experts estimate that in a major conflict 1,500 shiploads of oil per month would have to arrive in Western Europe to meet military and civilian needs.

This would mean a return to the large convoys of World War II, because large convoys afford better control and coordination and an efficient use of defensive resources. The use of convoys also forces submarines to come to the protected convoys and fight on terms of the convoy commander's choosing. A lesson from World War II: dispersing a convoy over a larger area means fewer ships sunk by submarines; at first ships were positioned at half-mile intervals; increasing the intervals to one mile cut losses by 25 percent.

Modern antisubmarine-warfare equipment and techniques permit even greater spacing today. A convoy of forty ships spaced at two-mile intervals would cover an area of 750 square miles. This also would make the convoy much less vulnerable to attack by tactical nuclear weapons.

A convoy can be protected by its own escort or else by sailing through an area tactically dominated by other friendly forces. The second method is a more efficient use of naval forces.

A convoy support group would include ships with towed arrays, helicopters, LRMP aircraft, and one or more SSBN submarines. Such a group would use passive sonar in an area ahead of the convoy unhampered by the underwater noise of the convoy. The convoy would proceed on a zigzag course, confusing enemy submarines and making it harder for them to get into attack positions.

A submarine commander must know what is happening on the surface before he can attack, and many obstacles stand in his way. The information from satellite or air reconnaissance will be out of date by the time it is passed on to him. If he runs at top speed to intercept the convoy, his chances of being detected rise sharply. Once there, his sonar may be confused, either by the sheer underwater noise of the convoy or by acoustic deception equipment. If he goes near the surface to use his radar or periscope, he almost certainly will be detected.

Submarines armed with cruise missiles do not need to approach a convoy as closely as those armed only with torpedoes. The Soviet Echo submarines carry the SS-N-3 Shaddock missiles with an estimated range of up to three hundred nautical miles, but they have to surface to fire them. The Soviet Charlie-class submarines can launch their SS-N-9 Siren missiles underwater, but they have an estimated top range of only one hundred miles.

In the event of a missile attack, electronic countermeasures cut down the chances of direct hits. Whether the threat is from submarines armed with torpedoes or missiles, the defensive strategy remains the same: confuse the submarine commander, force him to show himself, then destroy him. Once detected, a submarine should be destroyed before it can attack.

The most efficient way to turn a vague long-distance submarine contact into a target is by the use of aircraft. And submarines rarely are able to detect incoming aircraft until it is too late. The maritime patrol aircraft (MPA) is a workhorse of antisubmarine warfare with a special package of weapons, sensors, and target analysis equipment. The U.S. Navy's Lockheed S-3A Viking is carrier-based, but most current MPAs are land-based.

These planes carry magnetic anomaly detection (MAD) equipment, which is used to give a positive confirmation of an enemy submarine detection. The new Soviet submarines with titanium hulls are impervious to MAD. The plane's radars and infrared devices can pick up a

To minimize the amount of time that submarines must spend in port, tenders such as the *Simon Lake* carry supplies and the technicians and equipment needed to perform most repairs while on the high seas.

**Huge Soviet Oscar-class cruise
missile submarines were spe-
cially developed to take up a
position in advance of a U.S.
Navy carrier battle group and
launch a multimissile strike at
maximum range.**

submarine's exposed periscope at great distances. Radar profiles can
be displayed, giving instantaneous identification of the target. A
bathythermograph buoy often is dropped to check on the salinity of
the ocean, information which can be programmed into sonobuoys to
make them more accurate. Sonobuoys can be set to operate at different depths in active or passive modes, directional or omnidirectional.

Aboard the plane a computerized central tactical system correlates
data from the sensors, proposes weapon systems, and conducts the
release of weapons. MPAs carry various types of torpedoes and depth
bombs, armed with either nuclear or conventional warheads.

MPAs can operate independently or in support of a convoy, where
they will be deployed as part of the defensive screen. They often operate in conjunction with antisubmarine helicopters from ships protecting the convoy. When assigned to area search tasks, MPAs operate
independently, usually under a shore-based command.

Helicopters play an important role in protecting convoys because
they can operate off small surface ships. Initially helicopters were
considered extensions of the ship's sensor and weapon delivery systems, but they have evolved into fully autonomous antisubmarine
hunter-killers armed with homing torpedoes and depth bombs.

The ASW helicopter carries a dunking sonar, a unique surveillance
device that often is more effective than a sonobuoy because it can be
lowered through the sonar-deflecting thermocline to home in on oth-
erwise undetectable targets. The passive mode is used on dunking
sonar if it is believed that the submarine doesn't suspect it has been
detected; the active mode when the submarine is moving into an attack
position. Helicopters usually work in pairs, one working the dunking
sonar, the other ready to attack.

To sense the grand strategy of submarine and antisubmarine warfare it is instructive to look at the Greenland-Iceland-United Kingdom (GIUK) gap. Military experts believe that in an East-West conflict ships and submarines of the Soviet Northern Fleet would attempt to break out of northern waters into the Atlantic through the GIUK gap, while other Soviet ships and submarines would try to reach the North Sea through the Skagerrak, the waters separating Norway and Sweden from Denmark.

NATO considers both the GIUK gap and the Skagerrak choke points and has taken measures to seal them up. This involves fixed monitoring devices like seabed sonar, augmented by patrolling submarines, and ASW aircraft. Should a war seem imminent, U.S. and NATO forces would undoubtedly enter the area. (This scenario is the basis of Tom Clancy's novel *Red Storm Rising,* which imagines a nonnuclear East-West war.)

The Soviets have been conducting naval exercises for nearly a decade in the Norwegian Sea, the GIUK gap, and the waters to the west of the British Isles. These exercises are both a rehearsal for a breakout into the Atlantic and a response to the deployment of an amphibious force, NATO's announced plan in the event of a crisis on the northern flank. The Soviet Navy in 1985 reportedly set up submarine barriers in a number of areas, notably southeast of Iceland. Should war come, the stage is set for a major underwater battle there.

CHAPTER 11

"The hemorrhage of navy secrets"

Submarines are shrouded in secrecy, and when it is breached the results can be disastrous. In World War II a captured Enigma code machine enabled the British to monitor German U-boat activity. American cryptoanalysts built a replica of the Japanese cipher machine, cracked the naval code, and learned of the coming attack on Midway. The Russians scored a similar coup in the Cold War, not by brilliant intelligence work but by luck. A greedy American sailor simply sold them the submarine secrets they craved.

In January 1968 John Anthony Walker, Jr., a Navy chief warrant officer dressed in civilian clothes, approached the Soviet embassy in Washington, asked to talk to someone from security, and was ushered into the office of a KGB officer.

Walker carried with him a package containing the key settings for one of the Navy's top secret cipher machines. He said he could deliver complete data on the various cipher systems the Navy used to communicate with submarines and naval installations in Europe, and with submarines and surface ships deployed in the Atlantic. Walker was given several thousand dollars, and a clandestine meeting was arranged for the next month.

So began the bizarre Walker spy ring that would flourish for seventeen years and hand the Soviets more than a million top secret

Navy communications and the keys to decipher them. It was the greatest American espionage disaster since World War II. A Soviet KGB defector, Vitaly Yurchenko, said in his debriefing that if there had been a war during the period Walker was furnishing material, the Soviets would have won it.

When Walker began his career as a spy he was a communications specialist at COMSUBLANT (Commander Submarines Atlantic) in Norfolk. He had served on nuclear submarines, rising from seaman to warrant officer, a rank that gave him most of the perquisites of a commissioned officer.

In 1970 he was posted to the Navy communications school in San Diego as director of the practical applications laboratory. One of his students was Jerry Whitworth, whom he later recruited to supply secret material.

The other members of the ring included his brother Arthur, a lieutenant commander, who spent most of his Navy career in submarines until his retirement in 1973, and John's son Michael, who he talked into joining the Navy and specializing in communications.

Arthur supplied material from the Navy and later from his position at a shipyard doing contract work for the Navy. Michael stole documents from the carrier *Nimitz* and gave them to his father. John tried unsuccessfully to recruit his daughter Margaret, a civilian communications specialist with access to important material.

It truly was a family affair. John's wife, Barbara, learned what he was up to, a discovery that led to their divorce in 1976. The knowledge that John was a traitor had been too much for her to bear. Tortured by guilt, she developed a problem with alcohol. Several times she called the FBI but hung up as soon as someone answered.

John Walker, fearful that the Navy would uncover his activities, retired in 1976 and went into business as a private detective in Norfolk. Now he was selling the KGB information from Whitworth and, to a lesser extent, from his brother and his son.

John went to Casablanca and several times to Vienna to meet with the KGB to discuss the operation. The material and money were exchanged in elaborate "drops" in the Virginia countryside near Washington. He enjoyed the cloak-and-dagger aspects of the operation, and liked to think of himself as a master spy.

Finally, on November 17, 1984, Barbara Walker found the strength to tell the FBI that John was a spy. The FBI didn't think much of her story and for some months did nothing. Several times the case came close to being dropped.

The following spring the FBI decided it had a case. John, Arthur, and Michael Walker and Jerry Whitworth were arrested and charged with espionage. Michael was arrested on the carrier *Nimitz* in the Mediterranean and was returned under guard.

John plea-bargained, agreeing to testify against Whitworth in return for a reduced sentence for his son. John and Michael pleaded guilty to treason and were sentenced to life imprisonment and twenty-five

Part of the Walker spy ring, former Navy radioman Jerry Whitworth was convicted of selling naval code secrets to the Soviets for $332,000. The case was the largest security breach since World War II.

years, respectively. Arthur Walker and Whitworth were found guilty and given life sentences. There is no possibility of parole for persons convicted of treason.

Experts believe that the intelligence supplied by the Walker ring probably cost American lives in Vietnam, in addition to seriously compromising the submarine command. In his book on the case, *Breaking the Ring,* veteran investigative reporter John Barron made an assessment of the damage done to the Navy by the Walker spy ring:

"There is no doubt that the unveiling of virtually all navy secrets contributed significantly to the development of the modern Soviet navy and the diminution of the U.S. technological lead in important spheres. The first ships of the new Soviet navy began coming into service about the time John Walker began the hemorrhage of navy secrets. Therefore, the Soviets were able to study and learn at their convenience from the world's best teacher: the U.S. Navy."

Rear Admiral William O. Studeman, director of the Office of Naval Intelligence, in an affidavit submitted at the trial stated that the defendants "jeopardized the backbone of this country's national defense. Recovering from [this] espionage will take years and millions of taxpayers dollars. Even given these expenditures, we will likely never know the true extent to which our capabilities have been impaired."

In the wake of the Walker revelations, the Navy's submarine fleet has been a matter of growing concern to the defense establishment and Congress. Since the 1970s the Soviet Union has had the largest attack submarine force in the world, and has continued to build them at a rate faster than the United States. In the last decade the Soviets have developed thirteen new classes of submarines. The U.S. Navy has not developed a new class since the Los Angeles class in 1970. The Soviets today hold a three-to-one edge in numbers of fast attack submarines under the sea.

This advantage used to be largely discounted by the Navy because Soviet nuclear submarines traditionally were noisy. A hundred stealthy American attack submarines, the Navy said, could find and sink more than three hundred noisy Soviet submarines.

The day of reckoning came in 1987. An American spy satellite detected a new submarine at the Komsomolsk shipyard on the east coast of the Soviet Union. An American attack submarine monitored its sea trials in the Sea of Japan. When the audio and computer tapes of the new submarine were analyzed, Navy experts were stunned to find that the Soviets apparently had mastered the art of building quieter submarines. Their technology had leapfrogged ten years.

The new 360-foot submarine was the first of the Akula (Russian for shark) class, one of four new classes to become operational in the past few years. Anthony Battisda, formerly on the staff of the House Armed Forces Committee and a top submarine expert said, "The Akula is the best submarine in the water today." Some submariners cynically refer to the Akula as the first "Walker class" submarine. It is hard to imagine how the Soviets could use the information obtained from Walker to build a submarine *better* than the best U.S. submarines, but the comment is not without substance.

There is more disquieting news. The Soviets, apparently aided by the illegal sale from a Japanese firm of advanced Western technology for precision metal fabrication, are mass-producing superquiet submarine propellers and putting them on both new and existing submarines.

In 1983 U.S. intelligence rated 77 percent of Soviet submarines as noisy. Now it is believed that by the turn of the century 83 per cent of Soviet submarines will be rated quiet or very quiet. Russian naval officials predict that soon Soviet submarines will travel at fifty to sixty knots and operate down to 6,000 feet. The U.S. Navy discounts the Soviet claims, but admits it isn't even close to achieving similar performance goals.

Countering this Soviet threat is the primary mission of U.S. fast attack submarines, currently four diesel-powered and one hundred nuclear submarines, including thirty-eight of the Los Angeles class. Eighteen more Los Angeles-class submarines have been authorized, and the construction of a new class, Seawolf (SSN 21), began in 1989. This, the Navy believes, will "maintain its qualitative lead over the Soviet submarine force well into the twenty-first century."

Not everyone agrees. The first five submarines of the Seawolf class will cost nearly ten billion dollars; twenty-five more will cost another thirty billion. Some critics feel the money would be better spent by building more of the improved Los Angeles class, such as the San Juan. But neither the San Juan nor the Seawolf can come close to matching the performance characteristics of the Akula.

Other critics say that even the Los Angeles class is too big and too expensive. One Los Angeles-class submarine costs about twice as much as her British counterpart, the Trafalgar, and isn't nearly twice as good. They suggest that building more, less expensive fast attack submarines might be a more effective counter to the Soviet threat.

The Soviet Akula-class attack submarines were called the first of the "Walker class" submarines because they are believed to incorporate new technology sold to the Soviets by the Walker spy ring.

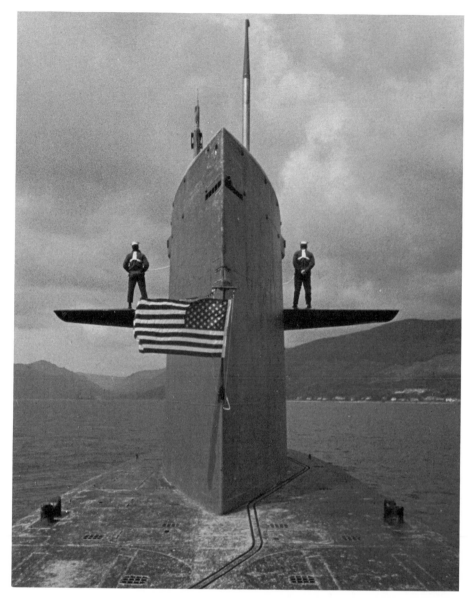

Sailors stand on the sail planes of the ballistic submarine *John C. Calhoun* as she enters the U.S. submarine base in Holy Loch, Scotland.

Concerned about these developments, Congress has appropriated one hundred million dollars for research on new underwater technologies. The Navy didn't ask for the money, and voiced strong objections to the appropriation. The Navy wants the Seawolf program, unshakable in the belief that it will prove effective against the best the Soviet has to offer. It may be well into the next century before anyone knows if the Navy's gamble will pay off.

The Navy and the Submarine Service have another problem. In the late 1960s the Navy had 980 active ships and some 78,000 officers and 600,000 enlisted men. Today with fewer than 600 ships there are about 74,000 officers and 523,000 enlisted men. And the ships now in service require fewer men to operate them than those of twenty years ago. While the Navy's size has been cut by 40 percent, its manpower is virtually unchanged.

This means, for one thing, too many officers chasing too few commands. And commanders spending too few years at the helm because of pressure from below. In the debates on military appropriations it rarely is mentioned that the majority of military costs are manpower costs. It is as if the military were simply a collection of weapons. Tom Clancy, writing in the *Washington Post,* summed up the problem and the solution this way:

"The military needs to restore the warrior ethic. Not all officers are or can be warriors, but only those who are deserve to command at any level. The military must change its programs to identify them, to nurture them, to select only the best from their ranks, and then to give them the support and the experience they need to fulfill their command responsibility. This will give us the force that will win in war; and recognition of it will go far towards preventing one."

Meanwhile, the deadly game of hide-and-seek in the depths of the ocean goes on and on.

Afterword

The threat of missiles launched in wartime from a nuclear submarine became a reality in the Persian Gulf. On January 18, 1991 the Los Angeles-class fast attack submarine, the U.S.S. *Louisville,* launched Tomahawk Cruise missiles armed with conventional warheads from her missile tubes against land targets in Iraq. Announcing the firing the following day, the Navy noted the historical nature of the event but declined to comment on the future use of nuclear submarines in the Gulf War.

Bibliography

Barron, John. *Breaking the Ring: The Bizarre Case of the Walker Family Spy Ring.* Boston: Houghton Mifflin Company, 1987.

Beach, Capt. Edward L. (Ret.). *The United States Navy: 200 Years.* New York: Henry Holt and Company, 1986.

Beebe, William. *Half Mile Down.* New York: Duell, Sloan & Pearce, Inc., 1934.

Burgess, Robert F. *Ships Beneath the Sea: A History of Subs and Submersibles.* New York: McGraw-Hill Book Company, 1975.

Campbell, Christy. *Weapons of War: Present and Future Weapons, Systems and Strategies.* New York: Peter Bedrick Books, 1983.

Carlucci, Frank C. *Annual Report to the Congress, Fiscal Year 1989.* Washington, D.C.: Department of Defense, U.S. Government Printing Office, 1988.

Carlucci, Frank C. *Soviet Military Power: An Assessment of the Threat.* Washington, D.C.: Department of Defense, U.S. Government Printing Office, 1988.

Carter, Jimmy. *Why Not the Best?* New York: Bantam, 1976.

Chief of Naval Operations, Office of. *Understanding Soviet Naval Developments.* Washington, D.C.: Department of the Navy, U.S. Government Printing Office, 1985.

Piccard, Jacques. *The Sun Beneath the Sea.* New York: Charles Scribner's Sons, 1971.

Polmar, Norman, and Allen, Thomas B. *Rickover: Controversy and Genius.* New York: Simon and Schuster, 1982.

Preston, Anthony. *Submarines.* New York: St. Martin's Press, Inc. 1982.

Roscoe, Theodore. *Submarine Operations in World War II.* Boston: Little Brown, 1972.

Sulzberger, C. S. *The American Heritage History of World War II.* New York: Bonanza Books, 1966.

Sweeney, James B. *A Pictorial History of Oceanographic Submersibles.* New York: Crown Publishers, Inc., 1970.

Verne, Jules. *Twenty Thousand Leagues Under the Sea.* New York: The Heritage Press, 1956.

Wyckoff, James. *Who Really Invented the Submarine?* New York: G. P. Putnam's Sons, 1965.

Photo credits